Dewey Decimal Classification,
21st Edition

Dewey Decimal Classification, 21st Edition

A Study Manual and Number Building Guide

Mona L. Scott

A Member of the Greenwood Publishing Group

Westport, Connecticut • London

This book is dedicated to

John Phillip Comaromi,
the editor of the 20th edition of the Dewey Decimal Classification,
as well as the Abridged 12th edition,
the previous edition of this manual, and dozens of other works on the DDC.

Libraries Unlimited
A member of Greenwood Publishing Group, Inc.
88 Post Road West,
Westport, CT 06881
www.lu.com

Dewey Decimal Classification, Edition 21
© 1996 by OCLC Forest Press, excerpts reprinted with permission.

Production Editor: Stephen Haenel
Copy Editor: Eloise L. Kinney
Proofreader: Lori Kranz
Typesetter: Michael Florman

Library of Congress Cataloging-in-Publication Data

Scott, Mona L.
    Dewey decimal classification, 21st edition : a study manual and number building guide / Mona L. Scott.
    ix, 198 p. 17x25 cm.
    ISBN 1-56308-598-4
    1. Classification, Dewey Decimal. I. Title.
Z696.D7S36 1998
025.4'31--dc21   98-6948
                                      CIP

10 9 8 7 6 5 4 3 2   EBAA 04 03 02

Contents

Preface

This work is a comprehensive guide to Edition 21 of the *Dewey Decimal Classification (DDC 21)*. The previous edition was edited by John Phillip Comaromi, who also was the editor of *DDC 20* and thus was able to impart in its pages information about the inner workings of the Decimal Classification Editorial Policy Committee, which guides the Classification's development. The manual begins with a brief history of the development of Dewey Decimal Classification (DDC) up to this edition and its impact internationally. It continues on to a review of the general structure of DDC and the 21st edition in particular, with emphasis on the framework ("Hierarchical Order," "Centered Entries") that aids the classifier in its use.

An extensive part of this manual is an in-depth review of how DDC is updated with each edition, such as reductions and expansions, and detailed lists of such changes in each table and class. Each citation of a change indicates the previous location of the topic, usually in parentheses but also in textual explanations ("moved from 248.463"). A brief discussion of the topic moved or added provides substance to what otherwise would be lists of numbers. Where the changes are so dramatic that a new class or division structure has been developed, Comparative and Equivalence Tables are provided in volume 1 of *DDC 21* (such as Life sciences in 560-590); any such list in this manual would only be redundant. In these cases, the only references to changes in this work are those topics that were moved from other classes.

Besides these citations of changes, each class is introduced with a brief background discussion about its development or structure or both to familiarize the user with it.

A new aspect in this edition of the DDC study manual is that it is combined with Marty Bloomberg and Hans Weber's *An Introduction to Classification and Number Building in Dewey* (Libraries Unlimited, 1976) to provide a complete reference for the application of DDC. Detailed examples of number building for each class will guide the classifier through the process that results in classifications for particular works within that class. In addition, at the end of each chapter, lists of book summaries are given as exercises in number analysis, with Library of Congress–assigned classifications to provide benchmarks.

The last chapter covers book, or author, numbers, which—combined with the classification and often the date—provide unique call numbers for circulation and shelf arrangement. Guidelines in the application of Cutter tables and Library of Congress author numbers complete this comprehensive reference to the use of *DDC 21*.

As with all such works, this was a tremendous undertaking, which coincided with the author completing a new edition of *Conversion Tables: LC-Dewey, Dewey-LC* (Libraries Unlimited, forthcoming). Helping hands are always welcome in our human existence, and this book is no exception. Grateful thanks are extended to Jane Riddle, at the NASA Goddard Space Flight Center Library, and to Darryl Hines, at SANAD Support Technologies, Inc., for their kind assistance in the completion of this study manual.

DDC:
History and Current Status

Edition 21 of the Dewey Decimal Classification (DDC) displays the continuous revitalization efforts that have kept it contemporary throughout the twentieth century. Progress in science, technology, and even thought and culture is consistently reflected within the classification. For this reason, its use by catalogers continues to grow nationally and internationally. (Table 1.1 at the end of this chapter charts the growth of the unabridged DDC's elements.)

The Modern History of DDC

The quarter century following Melvil Dewey's death in 1931 was one of "change and uncertainty" (Comaromi 1976, 339). After 60 years of close personal interaction, Dewey's loyal editorial team dissolved almost simultaneously with publication of *DDC 13* (1932). That edition continued the trend toward enumerative expansion upon existing number assignments. Nearly one-third larger than its predecessor, vilified for its corpulence, it still missed the equitable growth of all sections that many users wanted.

After considerable jockeying for control, a new editor took charge halfway through preparations for *DDC 14* (1942), but he lasted only until it was published. Questions of copyright, spelling, schedule proliferation, and cooperation with the International Institute of Bibliography shadowed that work. Its express goal was to develop all as yet unexpanded portions. Demand was growing for a "standard" edition that could serve the needs of an average-sized library of fewer than 200,000 volumes. It would bridge the gap between an intricately detailed bibliographic edition for large institutions, or for indexing purposes, and an abridged edition for school and small public libraries. *DDC 14* was intended to provide a comprehensive support for the controlled reductions anticipated in the forthcoming standard edition. It missed its publication deadline by a year, still failing to provide complete and uniform expansion. Nevertheless, it was a popular, unexpectedly long-lived edition.

However, what *DDC 17* called "slot-ification," or "classification by attraction," reached its zenith in the enumerations of *DDC 14* (Butcher 1979, 8). Subsequent editions increased synthetic modular devices such as auxiliary and precedence tables. Partly because of the enormous growth of factual knowledge,

1

simple enumeration could not satisfy the requirements of literary warrant (Matthews 1971, 572–77). The DDC Glossary notes that facets are based on characteristics of division.

When the standard edition appeared in 1951 it was, at best, a qualified success. Theorists said it abandoned or obscured the logical principle of development from the general to the specific. Its index was drastically reduced. It had less in common with *DDC 14* than was predicted. On the other hand, it cut out much deadwood, curtailed the troublesome simplified spelling, and introduced welcome modern terminology. A revised *DDC 15* appeared in 1953 with expanded form divisions, a considerably lengthened index, and other modifications. But irreversible antipathy curtailed sales, and accelerated the trend to reclassify from DDC to the Library of Congress scheme.

Caught in acute financial distress, the Lake Placid Club Education Foundation appealed to "outsiders" to help its programs. For instance, it solicited both the American Library Association and the Library of Congress for professional input. In late 1953, the Forest Press, its operational branch, contracted the Library of Congress to do the editorial work on schedule, and according to predetermined criteria. A use survey was made

> to determine whether librarians preferred integrity of numbers (fourteenth edition) or keeping pace with knowledge (fifteenth edition) for their basic policy of classification and to see what had been done in the cases of 316 specific relocations (Comaromi 1976, 419).

The result led to putting DDC numbers from both editions on LC printed cards, and set a more or less consistent policy for future development (Bulletin 1951, 1). The resuscitation was partly the work of new editor Ben Custer. However, most basic policy decisions had been made when he assumed charge in September 1956.

The modern history of DDC is generally dated from 1958, with publication of a refocussed Edition 16 that emphasized continuity and disciplinary integrity. Changes were kept to a minimum, reflecting only those most urgently needed to accommodate existing knowledge and literary warrant. Wherever possible, specific numbers were left vacant when discontinued. Only the 546–547 (Inorganic and Organic chemistry) sections were fully recast, inaugurating the overhaul in each successive edition of limited portions that were especially inadequate or unpopular (Dewey 1958, 23). Dewey's idiosyncratic spelling almost disappeared. Instructional notes were polished and multiplied.

Critics, especially in foreign countries, still found fault. The American Protestant bias remained, although the editors had worked to reduce it. Enumeration prevailed over rudimentary faceting for composite subjects. Users had trouble classing comprehensive works, especially where the decimal notation no longer reflected hierarchical subdivision. Nevertheless, the proof of the pudding was in the marketing. *DDC 16* may not have been a classifier's nirvana, but it sold like hot cakes, assuring the solvency of Forest Press and ensuring a systematic production schedule for later editions. A seven- to eight-year revision cycle was established. *DDC 17* came out in 1965. Its editor's introduction emphasized new or renewed emphasis on subject integrity and subject relationships, on the fundamental process of classification as distinct from what has been called "slot-ification."

Encouraged by Melvil Dewey's notable preference for practicality over theory in all activities, misled by the common American view of classification as little more than a system for assigning each book a convenient address or "slot" at which it can be stored and from which it can be retrieved, influenst [*sic*] by the failure of earlier editions of the DDC to provide under every discipline an expansion as full as was warranted by the literature acquired by libraries, classifiers of the past many times unwittingly abandoned the most fundamental feature of the system.... Unfortunately ... Edition 16 affirmed for the first time various practices that had grown up contrary to the consistent development of subjects by discipline (Dewey 1965, 43, 46).

While continuing to call its approach enumerative, *DDC 17* took a long step toward faceted number synthesis by expanding the table of form divisions, renaming it the "Table of Standard Subdivisions," and adding an "Area Table" which freed class 900 from its burden of enumerative detail, liberating geographic and political specifications from their traditional American distortion. "Divide like" and "Add area notation" instructions directed users to number sequences where established patterns of subdivision could be applied to different but related disciplines. The number of relocations was again reduced, although it still exceeded the announced limitation of 500. As for "completely remodeled schedules," the only explicit one was 150 (Psychology), which incorporated much of the material formerly located in class 130. Incidentally, the editor elsewhere cited Sections 614 (Public health) and 616 (Medicine) as areas of major relocation activity (Custer 1965, 557).

The Index gave trouble. It represented a 40 percent reduction of class number entries, but an enormous increase in cross-references. The editor later said of it:

Previous indexes had contained entries chiefly for those topics that were named in the schedules, plus significant synonyms and subtopics, but had supplied numbers only for those aspects where the topics were named, making no effort to guide the classifier to the vast hidden resources of the system.... The new seventeenth index provided full information for only a limited number of broad core concepts, referred to these from more specific topics, and made many "scatter" references to remind the classifier of other aspects.... This procedure called attention to many possibilities often previously overlooked, but frequently it did not supply a precise number that could be used without close scrutiny of the schedules. Because of the scarcity of exact numbers this index proved to be difficult and time consuming to use, and was replaced in 1967 by a conventional index (Custer 1972, 135).

Reminiscent of efforts to salvage the old standard edition, the new index was sent free with an apology to purchasers of the original *DDC 17*.

Preparation of this new index to Edition 17 is an emergency measure designed to meet the objections expressed in reviews, and is without prejudice to the form that may later be decided upon for the index to Edition 18 (Custer 1967, 59).

Even so, *DDC 17* was thought difficult to use. The editor's introduction, designed to replace the *Guide to Use of Dewey Decimal Classification* that accompanied *DDC 16*, was murky (Library of Congress, 1962). Instruction notes within the schedules were inadequate. Centered headings, meant to show the hierarchy, were confusing. The use of multiple zeros in synthetic numbers seemed impractical to many. Yet with all its shortcomings, real or imagined, sales topped those of *DDC 16* by 23 percent.

Problems of precedence, sequence, and relationship among topics represented by the notation are inevitable in a linear classification. Benjamin A. Custer's reemphasis on hierarchical development brought renewed concern for consistent handling of nuclear topics or their facets with respect to their disciplines or subjects. The Editor's introduction in *DDC 17* carried a new Section 3.354 on "Priorities of Arrangement." Its corresponding Section 3.555 in *DDC 18* adopted the more current name "Citation order" and carried a whole sequence of hints on modes of choice. The generalized instructions carried over into Section 8.55 of *DDC 19* with only minor revisions and expansions. They start with a reminder to check specific schedule tables and notes.

DDC 17 took a long step toward solutions at specific schedule points by introducing "Tables of Precedence." They were infrequent and experimental, but the operation proved successful, even though a few "patients died."

DDC 19 converted some minor tables into "order of precedence" notes. The number of such instructions has steadily increased, with elaborate schema now appearing in the Schedules proper, in auxiliary tables, and in the Manual. They are distinctively formatted with class numbers to the right of the headings.

The provision of options in DDC is a long-standing tradition. Dewey's introduction to *DDC 12* (1927), which was reprinted in later editions through the 18th, carried some suggested variations that could be applied to conform to local needs.

DDC 18, published in 1971 with an improved three-volume format, introduced the term "phoenix schedule" for its fully revised classes 340 (Law) and 510 (Mathematics). For ready reference, a reworked editor's introduction got its own index, and all relocations and discontinued numbers were tabulated. Five more auxiliary tables materialized. The older "Divide like" and "Add" notes were consolidated and simplified by listing a "base number" to which the extension could be added. Tables of precedence helped users determine citation order when building numbers. The Index curtailed its entries with class numbers, and increased its cross-references, but it was better received than the *DDC 17* Index.

Plans for the eighteenth edition included an enlarged index with all the traditional virtues plus a multiplicity of guides to hidden resources, therefore combining the good features and eliminating as far as possible the deficiencies of the two seventeenth edition indexes (Custer 1972, 7:140).

Foreign sales and translations steadily increased, while the flight from DDC to LC moderated. Dewey's brainchild had not yet exhausted its nine lives. Already in 1973, two years after publication, more copies of *DDC 18* had been sold than of any previous edition. Edition 20's early sales surpass even those of Edition 18.

DDC 19 continued the structure, style, and goals of *DDC 18*. The Index was difficult to use and usually unproductive. The revision of 301–307 Sociology was met by a storm of criticism. Forest Press brought out a revised and expanded version of 301–307 in 1982 to placate the critics. At the same time the Press published the *Manual on the Use of the Dewey Decimal Classification: Edition 19*, which was highly praised by the few who read it. (It would later become a part of Edition 20.)

DDC 20 continued the structure and goals of *DDC 19*. Its Index was not so difficult to use as its predecessor, but was usually as unproductive. The revision of 780 Music was met by discordant murmurs and widespread rejection. The completely revised introduction was appreciated by teachers and trainers. This edition was the first to be edited and available in a machine-readable form.

The appearance of *DDC 20* differed from that of immediately preceding editions, chiefly in its number of volumes (four) and its compressed layout. Increasing costs of paper and binding, together with a gradual but significant growth in the total number of entries, stimulated the search for a more compact product.

DDC 21 continues to reflect the needs of its users, especially those in foreign countries where criticism of the Protestant, Christian bias spurred major revisions in Religion. Tremendous strides were made in this direction by the consolidation of Christian aspects, thus bringing the classification more in line with that of other religions. The edition also continues the movement toward the structural emphasis on topics, as in Public administration and military science, which was revised to reflect the emphasis of first the topic, then the domain, rather than previously, where the domain was the structural emphasis under which the topics were found. The same is found in Life sciences, where the movement was from "organism/process to process/organism." Also in Life sciences, notations are simplified with "more specific and shorter numbers for fishes and mammals" (Dewey 1996, 1:xxiii).

An increase in cultural and social sensitivity resulted in changes in language used to describe various peoples, such as those with disabilities. The person precedes the affliction, where "physically handicapped persons" is replaced by "persons with physical disabilities" (Dewey 1996, 1:xx).

There is also a new number for "Collected persons treatment of members of specific racial, ethnic, national groups" (Dewey 1996, 32). Areas in which changes take place rapidly, such as computer science and country tables, are revised and/or expanded to depict the differences.

Lastly, *DDC 21* continues to become more user friendly, with strategically placed information, headings that are both more succinct and helpful, and the enlarged and enhanced Relative Index and Manual to assist in the selection of appropriate notations.

Forest Press/OCLC and the Editorial Policy Committee

As in the past, the Decimal Classification Editorial Policy Committee directed the course, and, under contract, the Decimal Classification Division of the Library of Congress completed the actual revisions of the classification. The Committee, composed of leaders in the field of classification from various backgrounds as well as from several different countries, provided the experience and wisdom that propelled the innovations found in major sections such as Religion, Education, Public administration and military science, and Life sciences in the *DDC 21*.

The day-to-day editing continues to be done on contract in the Decimal Classification Division of the Library of Congress. Benjamin A. Custer, chief of the division and editor of editions 16 through 19 and abridged editions 8 through 11, and to whom the 21st edition is dedicated, was a strong force in the revitalization of DDC. His successor for Edition 20, John Phillip Comaromi, continued the process of "de-slot-ification" that he had begun, repudiating Dewey's cynicism regarding logical structure and its dependence on verbal indexing. This concept supplements enumeration with structured citation orders and facet analysis (Custer 1980, 102) techniques that had developed chiefly in India and the United Kingdom.

Dewey Decimal Activities at the Library of Congress

The LC decision in the 1890s not to use the Dewey Decimal system in reorganizing its collections has been well documented. Whether Dewey himself, through his refusal to permit modifications, surrendered the balance of influence to Cutter's *Expansive Classification* is still being debated. At any rate, the shrewd Dewey decided that his scheme should have its numbers printed on LC cards. Early in 1925, he started a campaign to get them there. The officials at first dragged their feet, partly because of financial hurdles. However, Dewey's aversion for "no" and "impossible" finally co-opted the American Library Association, the Carnegie Corporation, and even the Library of Congress to help supply the money.

> The work of assigning class numbers began on April 1, 1930, and cards with numbers on them began to appear by the end of the second week in April. By Aug. 1 a staff of three began carrying out a program even broader than anticipated....
>
> The following classes of books currently cataloged by the Library of Congress are being assigned Decimal Classification numbers:
>
> (a) All books in English, with the exception of city directories, telephone directories, and nearly all current fiction.
>
> (b) Some foreign books, as many as the time of the present staff will permit.
>
> (c) Nearly all serial publications (*D.C. Numbers* 1930, 786–87).

But the Federal Connection was still a long way from satisfactory. After Constantin Mazney was dismissed in 1942, the editorship fell between the Decimal Classification Section of LC's Subject Cataloging Division and the Editorial Office, now also located in Washington, D.C. Weak financial support was probably a result, rather than a cause, of differences over developing the scheme as a whole, and over the kinds and quantity of materials for which LC would supply DDC numbers. At long last, in 1958, the two units merged (Bulletin 1958, 1). Still, the relatively low percentage of catalog records carrying DDC numbers decreased further during the early 1960s, when book publishing and library budgets accelerated more exuberantly than did the personnel available for processing. A second major influence in the flight from Dewey was the cost of determining DDC class and book numbers locally, as compared to adopting LC's ready-made call numbers. In 1967, an LC Processing Department reorganization elevated the Decimal Classification Office to division status, with a corresponding increase in staff and production.

Adding spectacularly to its direct service to libraries as a central source of DC numbers for specific works, the Division classed 74,335 titles, compared with 59,799 in 1967 and 35,000 in 1966. The 1968 coverage included all titles cataloged for the MARC program, all current (1966–1968) titles cataloged in English, and the more important and difficult current titles cataloged in the other major western European languages, and received through the National Program for Acquisitions and Cataloging (Welsh 1969, 189).

At a fiftieth anniversary party in May 1980, it was announced that 2,253,731 titles had "received DDC numbers for use by libraries everywhere and of every kind and size" (*Library of Congress Information* 1980, 243). Records with DDC numbers now run consistently over 100,000 per year.

The editing of all DDC editions after the 15th has been contracted to the Library of Congress. A copy of the agreement for producing *DDC 16* was published *in Cataloging Service*, to make users aware of developments (Bulletin 1954, 1–10). The Library's record of its Dewey assignments is the closest thing to a working shelflist that DDC editors have.

All editorial development work of the past twenty years, covering Editions 16 through 19, has included a careful check of the Library of Congress's Dewey-classed catalog to see the trends in the literature that require provision, and also, equally important, to see if the textual provisions of earlier editions, i.e., headings, definitions, scope notes, instructions, and the like, have been clearly enough expressed to be fully understood (Custer 1978, 84).

Functioning as a national library, LC can exchange information and enter into mutually beneficial agreements with foreign DDC users, as the following report shows.

Because thousands of users from Japan to Israel and Brazil to Mauritius utilize the Dewey decimal classification there is wide interest in its editorial development and in standardizing its application. Since 1969 the Decimal Classification Division has engaged in a lively exchange of information with the *British National Bibliography*, not only through transatlantic mail, which often moves weekly in each direction, but also through a six-week interchange of decimal classification specialists in 1972 as well as others with the *Australian National Bibliography* and *Canadiana*, the national bibliography of Canada. The result has been a common understanding of editorial policy, progress toward standardized interpretation of the schedules, and a vigorous expression of opinion and much give-and-take among four of the most important users of Dewey.

Recently the interchange with Great Britain entered a new dimension when British librarians, including the staff of BNB, undertook development of new schedules, subject to the guidance and review of the Decimal Classification Division. The first undertaking was the schedule for the new local administrative divisions of the United Kingdom that went into effect in April 1974. It will be followed by a revision of the Dewey decimal scheme for music. This type of dialogue has proved most useful and should be extended since through it overseas users obtain a more complete understanding of official Dewey policy and practice. In turn, they provide expertise in the development and application of the classification in fields of major concern to them (Library of Congress 1975, 23).

The serially published *Dewey Decimal Classification: Additions, Notes and Decisions,* usually called *"DC&,"* continues its supplemental updating services for Edition 21.

DDC's International Presence

The early American WASP bias in Dewey classification is well known. It was more or less inevitable, and even justifiable, in view of its clientele and the literary warrant of the time. But social change and the growing use of the system abroad sparked efforts to broaden its outlook. The decade of the mid-1960s to mid-1970s saw three major surveys of the impact of DDC outside North America, plus one on its use in the United States and Canada. These surveys were variously encouraged and partially financed by the Forest Press, the International Relations Office of ALA, the Library Association, the Asia Foundation, and the Council on Library Resources. Among other things they found:

1. Approval of techniques to give preferred treatment to local/national materials

2. Lack of enthusiasm for mixed notation

3. Concern over DDC's indifference to the "cuttering concept" or the use of book numbers

4. Some dissatisfaction with the order of the main classes

5. Criticism of numbers (usually synthetic) supplied in the index though not in the schedules

6. Lack of familiarity with *DC&* and consequent ignorance of schedule revisions prior to publication of each new edition

7. Desire for more information on DDC policies and revision plans

Concern for the non-English-speaking user dealt the coup de grâce to simplified spelling. *DDC 19* announced:

> a return to conventional American spelling from the residual simpler spellings of Editions 16–18, e.g., divorst, publisht, which greatly frustrated those whose native tongue is not English (Dewey 1979, 1:xxiii).

Celebration of the Dewey Centennial in 1976 stimulated a variety of cross-cultural activities such as the European Centenary Seminar at Banbury, England. British classificationists, who have long been interested in American schemes, have contributed penetrating commentary. The British serial *Catalogue & Index*, the English-language *International Classification* (published in Germany), and various foreign library association journals, particularly those in Canada, Australia, India, and South Africa, carry articles from time to time on DDC. Western European writers are particularly fond of comparing it to its FID-sponsored offspring, the Universal Decimal Classification (UDC). The studies do not usually redound to the praise of DDC, but they show more respect than they once did.

The appearance of DDC translations, sometimes abridged, or just as often locally expanded, is further evidence of DDC's international headway. With or without authorization, editions are available in such non-European languages as Hebrew, Thai, and Vietnamese.

Conclusion

The Dewey Decimal Classification is the protégé of a series of strong personalities who successively poured their energies into its infancy, development, maturity, and perpetuation. Melvil Dewey, Evelyn (May) Seymour, Dorkas Fellows, Milton Ferguson, David Haykin, and Ben Custer still cast atavistic shadows over *DDC 20*, shaping its inner consciousness and its outer presence. The advisory activities of the Editorial Policy Committee and the contractual services of LC's Decimal Classification Division have not essentially altered this paternalistic aspect. By contrast, the Library of Congress Classification, although originating in much the same social and intellectual climate, is the product of a series of subject specialists. The individual stamp of a Putnam, a Martel, or a Cutter is visible on a few general features and specific schedules, but the total effect of special interests competing for a viable compromise is reminiscent of much American governmental endeavor.

These derivations subtly affect public reaction to the two systems. The LC classification seldom inspires the enthusiastic personal commitment which is frequently accorded DDC. Proponents of the latter absorbed its rudiments in their school libraries, exploring its idiosyncrasies and learning to live with them as public or college library patrons. They are conditioned to its mnemonic, practical comprehensibility, and its broad comprehensiveness. LC advocates are generally more objective and sophisticated. They have likely come to learn the system as a kind of second language. They may know and prefer specific parts, but its sprawling multiplicity, its loose interrelations, and its lack of close integration through a comprehensive index leave them with little feeling of overall familiarity or identification.

As the present work will show, Edition 21 continues the pattern of development set by Custer with Edition 17.

Table 1.1
Growth of the Unabridged DDC's Elements*

Edition	Date	Table Pages	Schedule Pages	Index Pages	Total Pages	Editor
1	1876		10	18	42	M. Dewey
2	1885		176	86	314	M. Dewey
3	1888		215	185	416	M. Dewey
4	1891		222	186	471	M. Seymour
5	1894		222	186	471	M. Seymour
6	1899		255	241	612	M. Seymour
7	1911		408	315	779	M. Seymour
8	1913		419	332	850	M. Seymour
9	1915		452	334	856	M. Seymour
10	1919		504	358	940	M. Seymour
11	1922		539	366	990	D. Fellows
12	1927		670	477	1243	D. Fellows
13	1932	4	890	653	1647	D. Fellows
14	1942	4	1044	749	1927	C. Mazney
15	1951	1	467	191	716	M. Ferguson
15r	1952	1	457	400	927	G. Dewey
16	1958	5	1313	1003	2439	B. Custer
17	1965	249	1132	633	2153	B. Custer
17r	1967	249	1132	940	2439	B. Custer
18	1971	325	1165	1033	2718	B. Custer
19	1979	452	1574	1217	3385	B. Custer
20	1989	476	1804	726	3388	J. Comaromi
21	1996	515	2205	899	4037	J. Mitchell

*Although the table is helpful in seeing the progression of DDC, explanations are necessary to understand the figures completely. For example, the amount of information per page was not consistent; Edition 15's pages were spare, but Edition 14's were full and even compact at times. Edition 14 also was outsized on purpose to allow for the distillation of it for the Standard Edition. The elimination of "see-references" reduced the index pages in Edition 20 considerably. The inclusion of longer introductions and more and fuller tables, the incorporation of a manual, and other changes resulted in only three additional pages because it was far more compact than its predecessor.

Literature Cited

Bulletin. 1951. *Cataloging Service* 25: 1.

———. 1954. *Cataloging Service* 32: 1–10.

———. 1958. *Cataloging Service* 51: 1.

Butcher, Peter. 1979. Dewey? We sure do! *Catalogue & Index* 55: 8.

Comaromi, John Phillip. 1976. *The eighteen editions of the Dewey Decimal Classification.* Albany, NY: Forest Press Division, Lake Placid Education Foundation.

Custer, Benjamin A. 1965. Dewey 17: A preview and report to the profession. *Wilson Library Bulletin* 39 (7): 557.

———. 1967. Dewey lives. *Library Resources & Technical Services* 11 (1): 59.

———. 1972. Dewey Decimal Classification. In *Encyclopedia of library and information science.* Vol. 7. New York: Marcel Dekker.

———. 1978. The responsiveness of recent editions of the Dewey Decimal Classification to the needs of its users. In *General classification systems in a changing world.* The Hague: Fédération Internationale de Documentation (FID).

———. 1980. The view from the editor's chair. *Library Resources & Technical Services* 24 (2): 102.

D.C. numbers on L.C. cards. 1930. *Library Journal* 55 (17): 786–87.

Dewey, Melvil. 1958. *Dewey Decimal Classification and relative index.* 16th ed. Lake Placid Club, NY: Forest Press.

———. 1965. *Dewey Decimal Classification and relative index.* 17th ed. Lake Placid Club, NY: Forest Press.

———. 1979. *Dewey Decimal Classification and relative index.* 19th ed. Vol. 1. Albany, NY: Forest Press.

———. 1996. *Dewey Decimal Classification and relative index.* 21st ed. Vol. 1. Albany, NY: Forest Press.

Library of Congress. 1975. *Annual report of the Librarian of Congress for the fiscal year ending June 30, 1974.* Washington, DC: Library of Congress.

———. Decimal Classification Office. 1962. *Guide to use of Dewey Decimal Classification, based on the practice of the Decimal Classification Office at the Library of Congress.* Lake Placid Club, NY: Forest Press.

Library of Congress information bulletin. 1980. 39 (28): 243.

Matthews, W. E. 1971. Dewey 18: A preview and report. *Wilson Library Bulletin* 45 (6): 572–77.

Welsh, William J. 1969. The Processing Department of the Library of Congress in 1968. *Library Resources & Technical Services* 13 (2): 189.

▌▌▌▐ 2

General Aspects of the Dewey
Decimal Classification

Introduction

A discussion of DDC must be from two different points of view. One, *pure theory*, is how DDC looks at the world (knowledge) and then arranges it into a logical organization. The second is the *physical* structure of the classification, which supports the theory behind the organization of knowledge.

DDC's Theory of Knowledge

The theory behind the Dewey Decimal Classification is divided into four parts:

The realm of reason (wherein the mind attempts to understand itself and the spiritual and physical world outside itself): the sciences and the arts

The realm of imagination (wherein the mind produces literary inventions regarding life, no matter how much based in fact): belletristic literature, imaginative literature

The realm of memory (wherein the mind records events and conditions regarding the life of the planet and of humanity): geography, biography, history

Generalia (all other topics not included in the three "realms")

In general, the 800s take precedence over the rest of the classification; that is, a novel about conditions in the meat-packing industry of Chicago (e.g., *The Jungle* by Upton Sinclair) is classed in the 800s, not in meat packing in the 660s. *King Henry V* goes in English drama, not in English history. But a dialogue by Plato is classed in Philosophy in the 100s; an expository poem on the circulation of the blood, in Human physiology; a counting book in rhyme, in arithmetic. It is important to be careful in this first sorting of the nature of a work, especially when dealing with works for children.

The realm of reason (science) unfolds into philosophy, the source of systems for all other fields and the most general field of study. Theology, the science of the absolute and the ultimate field of philosophy, comes next. Religion, which is not scientific but is tributary to theology, is included in theology. As humankind achieves its most spiritual role within society and in relation to the state, the social

13

and political sciences are logically the next fields of study. The political sciences are jurisprudence—in which society puts constraints upon the individual—and politics—in which the individual reacts against the constraints of law, thereby perhaps producing an instance for an alteration of the practical will. The social sciences are political economy, whereby in combination humankind gains ascendancy over nature and uses it for personal ends, and education, by which humankind is initiated into the society's modus operandi. Placed at the end of the social and political sciences is philology, as it is the result of self-conscious thought, a society's best record of itself, and the connecting link between the spiritual and the natural. The natural sciences now follow, and these are followed by the useful and fine arts. The first unfold the laws of nature; the next applies them to social uses. The point of transition between them is medicine, which is part science and part art. This brings to an end the subjects whose major mode of treatment is the scientific.

The second realm collects works of the imagination: poetry, prose fiction, and so on.

The last realm is the historical. History comprises geography and travels, civil history, and biography and correspondence; heraldry and genealogy fall here.

A topic may fall into any of the three realms. Consider, for instance, the Library of Congress. One could write about it scientifically, explain its present and future role in intelligence gathering, estimate the date upon which it will be filled from top to bottom, delineate its effect upon the artistic life of America, describe the richer life of those who benefit from its program of talking books, and so on. One may say that these are not all scientific subjects. The assertion is uncontestable and inappropriate. It is the mode of discussion that is scientific, not the subject. One could write about the Library of Congress historically: examine its past role in intelligence gathering, investigate how long it took to build the Library of Congress Thomas Jefferson Building, list who helped in its construction, explain the source of the stone that makes up its walls, and so on. And, lastly, one could write about the Library of Congress artistically: devise a novel in which a descriptive cataloger spends his or her days in remembrance of things past, and is subsequently fired; or pen a poem about the institution, which brings an artistic aspect.

DDC's Structure (The Schedules)

A basic premise of DDC is that it is arranged by discipline and not by subject. This frequently presents problems in classifying materials, but the Relative Index's job is to alleviate such difficulties.

The next basic premise is that of "tens." The Schedules are arranged in ten classes, which are organized into ten divisions, each of which is divided into ten sections.

Each notation is made up of three basic numbers, which represent a particular place in the Schedules. The first digit indicates one of the ten classes. The second digit represents one of the ten divisions within the class. The third digit distinguishes one of the ten sections. Most notations require further refinement, so a decimal is inserted following this three-part number to be followed by more digits representing a specific element of the topic.

DDC notation remains traditionally pure. That is, it consists only of the arabic digits 0 through 9, plus the decimal point. The shortest possible number is three digits long, because lead zeros are written out in class 000.

Number columns, Schedules, Index, and Table numbers are printed in groups of three, for example, 629.133 340 422 (Private airplanes), and —772 33 (Vanderburgh County, Indiana). The groupings merely facilitate reading. In common practice, the spaces are removed when writing the numbers as classifications. Brackets indicate recently or permanently vacated locations.

Hierarchical Order

After the "slot-ification crisis" of Edition 16, the editorial policy has stressed disciplinary integrity, largely through the use of hierarchical subordination, or the logical progression from the general to the specific.

> The DDC is a hierarchical classification, which means that it develops progressively from the general to the specific in disciplinary and subject relationships. Even so, the overall arrangement is not necessarily theoretical or logical. The DDC is built on the premise that no one class can cover all aspects of a given subject (Bloomberg and Weber 1976, 17).

This suggests that the hierarchical structure is not necessarily a linear one. The editors of *DDC 20* claim that any specific class has two or three sets of relationships: coordinate, subordinate, and sometimes superordinate (Dewey 1989, 1:xxviii–xxix). However, this is basically a hierarchical system, which is more easily seen in the pure and applied sciences and is less evident in generalities, the humanities, or the social sciences.

This hierarchical or "tree" structure is echoed in the notation. Within this basic structure, the first level in the classification of an item is the first digit (Main Class); the second level of subdivision is the addition of the second digit (Division). The third level of subdivision (Section) is provided by the addition of the third digit added to the two previously selected digits.

3[00]	Social sciences	(Main Class)
34[0]	Law	(Division)
342	Constitutional and administrative law	(Section)

At this point, Summary tables provide overviews of the hierarchies.

342.001–.009	Standard subdivisions; laws, regulations, cases, procedures, courts
.02	Basic instruments of government
.03	Revision and amendment of basic instruments of government
.04	Structure, powers, functions of government
.05	Legislative branch of government
.06	Executive branch of government
.07	Election law
.08	Jurisdiction over persons

.09	Local government
.1	Socioeconomic regions
.3–9	Specific jurisdictions and areas

Centered Entries

Various subjects within the Schedules are encompassed in ranges of numbers. These entries are called *Centered Entries* because the range of numbers is centered on the page, with a > at the left margin.

> **342–349 Branches of law; laws (statutes) ...**

These Centered Entries are divided categories (*facets*), which are further divided by various characteristics. Each facet's specific notation is initiated by a digit, such as *0*, which often precedes a standard subdivision. (Historical, geographic, persons treatment is a standard subdivision.)

342.009	Historical, geographic, persons treatment
342.04	*Structure, powers, functions of government
342.041	Powers and functions of government
342.0418	*Police powers

The asterisk (*) beside the topic in the Schedules leads the user to a note at the bottom of the page:

*Add as instructed under 342–347

Broad and Close Classification

One of the most notable features of DDC is its adaptability to libraries of every size. Smaller libraries may shorten their notations where they find it prudent by eliminating detailed subdivisions and retaining only the main classes and subdivisions, which is referred to as broad classification. Larger libraries with more extensive collections generally use close classification and use all of the detailed subdivisions that are applicable.

Libraries may use any method of shortening the notations, but the accepted one is that offered by the Library of Congress, which segments the numbers with marks indicating appropriate breaks for shortened notations.

Relative Index

Although both the schedules and the index of a classification system match linguistic with notational representations of the concepts—or actually of the library materials—being classified, they have reciprocal functions, offering different insights. Schedules graph or delineate the structure, using notation to accent symmetries, analogies, and hierarchies. The Index offers random access through alphabetized primary and subordinated terms. Bloomberg and Weber (who quote the editors of *DDC 18*) offer the following evaluation:

No other feature of the DDC is more basic than this: that it scatters subjects by discipline (DDC, Vol. 1, p. 18). The Editor's Introduction to the DDC further states that "the primary basis for DDC arrangement and development of subjects is by discipline ... while subject, strictly speaking, is secondary" (DDC, Vol. 1, p. 17). One of the functions of classification is to bring together on the shelves materials on the same subject and on related subjects. It needs to be emphasized, however, that no classification accomplishes that function perfectly. It is important to remember that all material on a subject is seldom if ever classed together.... Thus, throughout the DDC various aspects of a topic or discipline may be placed in different numbers.... No attempt is made to place all aspects of a topic in one number in the schedule.... The device that brings together the various aspects and relationships of a topic is the Relative Index (1976, 20).

For example, Agriculture is listed in the Relative Index as follows:

Agriculture	630
applied science	630
economics	338.1
enterprises	338.763
law	343.076
public administration	354.5

Although all of the last four entries are related to Agriculture, they are actually in another class.

The backbone of the DDC Schedules are the disciplines, which are "organized fields of study or branches of knowledge" (Dewey 1996, 1:lix). These may be a class of DDC, such as Religion (200), or a division, such as Psychology (150). As illustrated above, the various subjects, or topics, are found in the Schedules within the disciplines. The Relative Index is a guide to subjects or topics associated with disciplines.

The Relative Index brings together the various aspects and relationships of a topic. It is an alphabetical listing of all the main headings in the DDC schedules, showing also synonyms and, to a large degree, the relation of each subject to other subjects. The DDC defines "relativity" as "that property of the index which reverses the subordination of subject to discipline, thus bringing together from all disciplines the various aspects of individual subjects" (DDC, Vol. 1, p. 60). Earlier it was pointed out that the DDC scatters aspects of subjects by discipline throughout the schedules. The Relative Index brings together the various aspects of a topic (Bloomberg and Weber 1976, 33).

In the Index, subjects are listed in alphabetical order, with lists of disciplines under which the subjects are found.

Law	340
information systems	025.063 4
literature	808.803 55

Many class numbers in the Index are not spelled out in the Schedules because they have been "synthesized," or built, from Add instructions. Using the example above, we find 025 is Operations of libraries, archives, information centers. Looking further we find the following:

.06   Information storage and retrieval systems devoted to specific disciplines and subjects

             Class here documentation of specific disciplines and subjects

[.060 001–.060 009] Standard subdivisions

             Do not use; class in 025.0401–025.0409

.060 01–.069 99   Specific disciplines and subjects

             Add to base number 025.06 notation 001–999 ...

There is no .063 4 indicated, but it seems to be included in .06001–.06999. Instructions indicate how to add numbers for the specific disciplines and subjects. In this case, 34 is added from the Schedules, indicating Law (340).

The search for a class number begins with the Relative Index, which lists *subjects* in alphabetical order with disciplines identified underneath (with their notations). Not all topics in the Schedules are in the Index, nor are all of the topics in the Index in the Schedules. They are implied, because the Schedules are not exhaustive. Some names from Table 2 are included (countries, states, and provinces of many countries, U.S. counties, capitals, and other important cities, important geographic characteristics) and heads of state that are often used to note historical periods.

Users are warned against assigning class numbers directly from the Index without examining their placement in the Schedules. For a satisfactory subject classification, it is necessary to verify the number within the context.

When Melvil Dewey produced the first edition of the DDC, he called the Index a "Subject Index," and that is exactly what it was. It was not an index of the terms found in the Schedules; it was a list of topics he thought to be important to the students and faculty of Amherst College.

A number on the same line as an Index term would naturally be thought to be for the *topic* given and thus for the *subject* being discussed in the work. This may or may not be true. The Relative Index is generally not a subject index—in Dewey's sense of the phrase—and it should not be confused with it.

The Manual

The Manual shares the last volume with the Relative Index, and both assist classifiers in their search for proper notations. The Manual is arranged in the same order as the Schedules, although not all numbers are found there because its purpose is to provide further explanations about the proper use of numbers that may present problems in understanding their use. Some examples follow:

362.1042 vs. 368.382
Social aspects [of health services] vs. Health insurance

570–590
   Biology
                        Number building

The first example guides the user in deciding under which of the two subjects the work being classified fits. At 362.1042 and 368.382 in the Schedules, there are instructions to *"See Manual at 362.1042 vs. 368.382."*

The second example is pages of instructions about how to add facet numbers, or numbers for the various aspects of biology. Following the introductory notes after "570 Life sciences   Biology" in the Schedules, there is a reference to *"See Manual at 560–590; also at 570–590: Number building; also at 578 vs. 304.2, 508, 910."* It is *always* important to refer to the Manual when instructions under a number indicate that there is an explanation in the number range the classifier uses. This is the only guarantee that the notation chosen will be the appropriate one.

Types of Changes Found in *DDC 21*

Controlled expansion, reduction, and relocation constitute the primary modes of change. DDC editors often combine them in varying formats to make the system more responsive to contemporary needs or to implement the goal of subject integrity from a modern perspective. What seems to be a small readjustment may turn out to be nearly as far-reaching, or just as controversial, as a sudden large one. Completely recast Schedules appear to be most revolutionary, but they differ only in degree, not in kind.

Tinkering with the Schedules is not the only way to modify a classification scheme. The semantic, and even the structural, peculiarities of the mediating language have their own laws and pose their own problems of change. In succeeding chapters, we shall examine syntactic and syndetic adjustments made in *DDC 21*.

Below, the types of expansions, reductions, and relocations are discussed and examples of each type are presented.

Expansions

Expansions introduce new numbers, or ones that had not been used recently, for one of six purposes.

1. Subdivision of a Class Number

A specific topic may have been included under a broad heading. The growth of knowledge or the increase in materials written on the subject now warrants giving it a place of its own.

Multimedia systems was shifted from 006.6, and assigned 006.7, a new number.

2. Extended Meanings for Standard Subdivisions

Deviations from Table 1 usage are often accompanied in the Schedules by notes referring to other sections of the Schedules.

Organizations under religion were moved from [.6] to 291.65.

3. Standard Subdivision Scatter

To improve subject integrity, materials formerly grouped together because of a common aspect are relocated throughout the Schedules by use of a standard subdivision.

Safety measures for particular excavation techniques were moved to the particular technique in 622.22–.29, with notation —0289 from Table 1 added.

4. Tables of Precedence

These tables help users choose among competing concepts in the course of synthesizing (building) numbers.

A Table at the beginning of Education (370) offers these instructions:

Unless other instructions are given, observe the following table of preference, e.g., special education at elementary level 371.90472 (*not* 372).

Public policy issues in education	379
Special education	371.9
Specific levels of education	372–374

5. Multiple 0s for Subdivision

In some areas, the single zeros are used for other kinds of subdivisions, so additional zeros are added to the standard subdivisions.

Under Oriental philosophy (181), the structure is

.001–.008	Standard subdivisions
.009	Historical treatment
.04–.09	Philosophies based on specific religions

6. New Concepts

The growth of knowledge, or library materials on a subject not previously available, results in new numbers added to the Schedules.

004.678 is a new number for the Internet.

Reductions

A reduction results from shifting one or more topics to a number shorter than the old but otherwise not differing from it. There are three reasons that this may occur.

1. Discontinued Number, or Total Reduction

If a new edition removed the entire contents of a number to a more general number, the original number is "discontinued." In the Schedules and Tables, the "reduced" numbers are bracketed with the note, "Number discontinued; class in...." The superordinate number may or may not name the old caption in a note.

> Geographic distribution of Labor force was moved from [331.111] to 331.1109.

2. Meaningless Content

This may occur when a topic no longer has any meaning within its context. Three are listed in Edition 21.

> Special topics under Religion [204] was discontinued because it is without meaning in the context of Religion here.

3. Partial Reduction

This results when a number loses only part of its meaning but is retained within this edition's Schedules. These numbers are not bracketed but will have instructions concerning the nonuse of the number for the given topic, including directions about where to class it.

> Election procedures was located under Voting procedures at 342.075 but was moved "upward" in the hierarchy:

.075   Voting procedures
            Use of this number for election procedures discontinued; class in 342.07

> The number is not bracketed and is retained for other meanings, such as "absentee voting."

Relocations

A relocation occurs when a topic is shifted to a number (other than to a superordinate number or in an expansion of the topic upon the same base number). The old number may be bracketed, indicating that it is vacated and its use discontinued in this edition. These shifts may result in consternation by the users of the Schedules, and so they are not done lightly. "Relocations ... are made for various reasons in DDC, to keep pace with new knowledge or to rectify some of the structural irregularities which have developed in the system over the years" (Chan 1973, 38).

Figures indicating the number of relocations in previous editions range from 100 in Edition 2 to 1,098 in the twentieth. But there has been no consistent method of counting them because with systematic faceting the exact total of discontinued numbers and relocations cannot be precisely stated, and the total is often disputed by even such authorities as Benjamin A. Custer and John Phillip Comaromi. In this work, no effort is made to develop a total number of relocations because that number is meaningless in relation to the effect on the various collections around the world. Some libraries, because of their focus, will experience little impact, but others may require the reclassing of vast sections of their holdings. In later chapters these relocations, as well as other alterations to the *DDC 20* Schedules, will be discussed in detail to assist the users in reconciling their collections. These locations are done in eight instances.

1. Total Relocation

    This occurs when a number has lost all of its meaning in its context; then it appears in this edition in brackets with a note beginning, *"formerly...."*

    > Armorial bearings and Comprehensive works on coats of arms were *both formerly* 929.82, but are now found at 929.6 under Heraldry.

2. Relocated Span

    In some cases, not just a single number but a whole span of numbers may be relocated.

    > In the overhaul of Life sciences, many whole spans were moved en masse; for example, Natural history of organisms and related subjects was moved from 574 to 578.

3. Relocation of Split Meanings

    Topics with single numbers or spans may be discontinued to have their meanings distributed elsewhere. These will be indicated with a series of relation notes separated by semicolons.

    > Management of personnel of specific ages and sexes (658.3042) is no longer used and all its "parts" moved elsewhere. ("Management of men relocated to 658.30081, management of women relocated to 658.30082," etc.)

4. Partial Relocation

    This results when the original number retains some of its meaning, losing only part to a different class number. Instructions at the old location refer the user to the new one, which is annotated by a bracketed note beginning *"formerly...."*

    > Acid rain was moved to 344.046336 from 344.04634, Pollution of specific environments, which is retained in the Schedules.

5. Split Relocation

    In some instances only part of the meaning of a topic will be shifted to various other places, leaving the topic also in its existing place.

    > Financial administration of agencies supporting public education had been included under Support of public education (379.11) but was moved to 353.824, leaving the rest of Support of public education in its former place.

6. Splitting Out Comprehensive Works

"Comprehensive works" are often shifted to a superordinate number or relocated completely to other hierarchies or other portions of their original hierarchy.

> Comprehensive works on mammals was moved from 333.959 to 333.954 (same hierarchy).

7. Scatter Relocation

When the meaning of the discontinued heading is dissipated so widely that full enumeration of its relocations would be impracticable, a general scatter note or its equivalent is given. Scattering is done to improve subject integrity.

> Instructional facilities for teaching specific subjects was under Laboratories (371.6234) but is now "Relocated to specific subject, e.g., language laboratories 407.8, chemical laboratories 542.1."

8. Hierarchical Force of Relocation

If a topic with subdivisions is relocated, the subdivisions are also relocated or discontinued altogether. Usually the hierarchy is retained, although not necessarily in the previous form.

> In the revamping of Religion (200), all of the standard subdivisions were moved en masse from the first division (201, 202, etc.) to the third (230).

Overview of *DDC 21* Revisions

As indicated in chapter 1, Edition 21 continues an evolutionary path of gradual changes to keep pace with the rapid growth of knowledge as well as the shrinking of the world that results from the swift exchange of information now capable through technology and the easy movement of people. In addition to those discussed in the last chapter, significant changes were made in the following areas.

- Education (370) has many revisions, including the revision and expansion of the subdivisions. The Education of women (376) and Schools and religion (377) are now subdivisions under 371. Home schools and schooling was also moved from 649.68 to 371.042.

- Insurance (368) was analyzed, revised, and expanded.

- Subdivisions for Christianity (201–209) were moved to 230–270 in continuing an effort to reduce Christian bias.

- Judaism (296) was revised and expanded. Options provide for the arrangement of the books of Tanakh according to Jewish tradition.

- Islam was also revised and expanded.

These and other changes are found detailed in succeeding chapters.

Literature Cited

Bloomberg, Marty, and Hans Weber. 1976. *An introduction to classification and number building in Dewey*. Ed. John Phillip Immroth. Littleton, CO: Libraries Unlimited.

Chan, Lois Mai. 1973. The tenth abridged DDC ... and children's room/school library collections. *School Library Journal* 20 (1): 38.

Dewey, Melvil. 1989. *Dewey Decimal Classification and Relative Index*. 20th ed. Vol. 1. Albany, NY: Forest Press.

———. 1996. *Dewey Decimal Classification and Relative Index*. 21st ed. Vols. 1, 2. Albany, NY: Forest Press.

3

Principles of Number Building

Introduction

Often, the subject of a work to be classed does not appear in either the Relative Index or the Schedules; thus, it is often necessary to *build* the required number for the classification of the work. The process begins with the base number, which is then added to according to instructions found in the Schedules. "Adding" numbers come from the seven Tables, Add Tables in the Schedules and other parts of the Schedules. Table 1 (Standard Subdivisions) notations can be added to any number in the Schedules unless there are specific directions not to use the standard subdivisions.

When more than one facet (aspect) is needed to class a work, a series of added numbers may be required. These numbers are added in "citation order" taken from a whole sequence of hints in the Schedules on methodologies of choosing the order of "adds." Where there are no instructions for adding more than one aspect, "preference order" is used. This is the order indicated in "preference" notes, or instructions in the Schedules proper, auxiliary Tables, and in the Manual.

Principles of Book Classification

Classifying books has been defined "as the art of assigning books to their proper places in a system of classification in which the various subjects of human inquiry, or the descriptions of human life in its various aspects, are grouped according to their likeness or relation to one another" (Merrill 1939, 1). In practice, however, this is not an easy task. Catalogers use the following nine general principles when selecting a DDC number:

1. Class a book, or any other material, where it will be most useful to the patron. This can usually be accomplished by placing similar materials together. This may also be accomplished by the use of broad or close classification, depending on library needs.

2. Class a book first by subject and second by form, except in the field of literature. For example, an encyclopedia of art will be classed in art and not with general encyclopedias. The subject, art, is more important than the form, an encyclopedia.

3. Class a work of literature first by its original language and second by its form. For example, a work on French poetry translated into English will be classed in the number for French poetry, not for English poetry, because the original language is French. After the original language of the work has been determined, it is then classed by form (drama, poetry, fiction, essays, speeches, and letters).

4. Class a book that covers two or three subjects under the *first* subject treated unless another subject receives more prominent attention. A book that treats first chemistry and then physics but that gives equal treatment to each is classed with the first subject treated, chemistry.

5. Class a book that covers more than three subjects in a general subject embracing all of the subjects. For example, a book treating mathematics, astronomy, physics, and chemistry will be classed with comprehensive works on pure science. A work treating arithmetic, algebra, trigonometry, and geometry is classed with comprehensive works on mathematics.

6. Class a book in the most specific number possible in the classification scheme. For example, a history of the American Civil War will be classed in a specific number for the Civil War and not in a more general number. A work on the banjo is classed in the specific number for the banjo and not in a general number for string instruments. Classifying a book in too general a number defeats the purpose of classification, because it places books on specific topics in meaningless order.

7. In general, class a book first by subject if there is a choice between subject and geographical location. For example, a book on German architecture is classed in the number for architecture, not in the number for geography of Germany.

8. Class biographies, autobiographies, diaries, and reminiscences either together in a general biography number or with specific disciplines. For example, a biography of a lawyer is classed either in a general number covering biographies of people regardless of occupation or in a number in law used for biographies of lawyers, judges, etc.

9. Class a book according to the author's intent in writing it. For example, if an author produces a book of drawings of dogs, the cataloger must examine the book to see if the book is meant to emphasize the different breeds or techniques of drawing dogs. Depending on the author's intent, the book could be classed in a number for dogs or a number for techniques of drawing (Bloomberg and Weber 1976, 39–40).

The Theory of Number Building

The foundation of number building is the base number, which is a sequence of numbers that does not vary but remains the same; digits from other parts of the Schedule or from the Tables can be added as instructed. For example, the base number for all languages is 4, and all numbers are added to base number 4. The base number for Tagalog (Filipino) is 499.211. Instructions tell the classifier to "Add to 499 the numbers following —99 in notation 991–999 from Table 6 ... then to the number for each language listed below add notation 01–8 from Table 4." Thus, in any sequence the *base* number does not vary (e.g., Dictionary of Tagalog is 499.2113, or 499.211 + 3 for dictionaries). It is from the base numbers that the classifier builds more specific numbers for the materials being cataloged. Number building is the process of developing a number by the addition of numbers or segments of numbers from other parts of the Schedule, from the Tables, or both.

Scope Notes, Class Here Notes

A "scope" note usually appears after a major classification number, stating exactly what is to be classed in the number.

> 543.0893   Ion-exchange chromatography
> Class here ion-exchange separations
>
> Class ion-exchange separations in liquid chromatography in 543.0894; class ion-exchange separations in gas chromatography in 543.0896

The first note defines the scope of the subject to be classed in the number. The second note suggests alternative numbers for more specialized aspects. Another example of a "scope" note is found at 333.954, the number for Animals as a natural resource under Economics.

> 333.954   Animals
> Including biomass energy, genetic resources, germ plasm
>
> Class here comprehensive works on mammals [*formerly* 339.959], on vertebrates; wildlife

The first note lists special topics also to be classified in the number. The second note is a "class here" note, which directs the classifier to use the 333.954 for comprehensive works on mammals, vertebrates, and wildlife.

An "add" note gives directions for building numbers for specialized subtopics.

> 294.33   Mythology, social theology, interreligious relations and attitudes
> Add to base number 294.33 the numbers following 291.1 in 291.13–291.17, e.g., social theology 294.337

In the example below, the first note defines the term, and the "class elsewhere" note gives directions relating to major aspects of a broader topic.

> 331.22   Compensation differentials
> Differences among industries, occupation, regions
>
> Including comparison among firms in the same industry
>
> Class determination of compensation, factors affecting compensation in 331.215

Always read all the notes before using a DDC number. The notes are essential for number building and for determining where to classify materials. Failure to read and carefully follow the notes in the DDC Schedules will result in incorrect classification or incorrectly built numbers.

Options

Recent emphasis on the international appeal of DDC, as well as its increased sensitivities to various peoples, has expanded the number of options offered. They are often found in parentheses at the beginning of a discipline. For our example of Law, three separate options are available (under 342–349) to give "preferred treatment to the law of a specific jurisdiction, to jurisdictions in general, to branch of law and its subordinate subjects, or to discipline or subject." Another example is Option B under 420–490 Specific languages, where letters of the alphabet can be used to shorten the number for a specific language. Options, however, are not recommended unless the local classifier finds cogent reasons for using them.

Adds

Facets, or categories, are governed by notes in the Schedules to "Add to" or "Add from." "Add tos" replace the previously used "Divide likes," which refer to Schedule shifts rather than Tables. An example follows.

342.04   *Structure, powers, functions of government

The asterisk (*) beside the topic in the Schedules leads the user to a note at the bottom of the page:

*Add as instructed under 342–347

In this particular part of the 300 class, there are two Tables: one for 342–349 inclusive and another for 342–347. Detailed instructions are found:

> 342–347 Branches of law

Class here comprehensive works on specific subjects of law.

Except for modifications shown under specific entries, add to each subdivision identified by * as follows:
01   Philosophy and theory
          [Etc.]

"Add froms" refer to the Tables found in Volume 1. Going back to the example above, for 342, Constitution and administrative law, the summary indicates the following:

342.001–009	Standard subdivisions; laws, regulations, cases, procedure, courts
.02	Basic instruments of government
.03	Revision and amendment of basic instruments of government
.04	Structure, powers, functions of government
.05	Legislative branch of government
.06	Executive branch of government
.07	Election law
.08	Jurisdiction over persons
.09	Local government

The standard subdivision 342.009 is for the Historical, geographic, persons treatment and refers to Table 1 in Volume 1. If 05 is added to the .009, the 21st century, 2000–2099, is indicated.

Tables

The seven Tables in the full DDC are important devices that aid in number building; they serve a mnemonic (memory) function. In the DDC the mnemonic feature involves using the same combination of numbers to represent the same topic or to have the same meaning throughout the Schedules. Thus, 05 means *periodicals* wherever it is added, which gives a consistency in meaning in various contexts. The numbers from the Tables are *never* used alone but always in conjunction with numbers from the classification Schedules. A dash (—) preceding the numbers emphasizes that they must be added to another number, but the dash is omitted when adding to a number.

Table 1. Standard Subdivisions

Standard subdivisions can be added to any number in the Schedules unless instructions in the Schedules indicate otherwise. These subdivisions provide notations to identify works that may be in a particular format or physical form (examples of treatment by format or physical form are dictionaries, encyclopedias, and periodicals), a historical or geographical approach, or a philosophical or theoretical perspective.

—01	Philosophy and theory
—02	Miscellany
—03	Dictionaries, encyclopedias, concordances
—04	Special topics
—05	Serial publications
—06	Organizations and management
—07	Education, research, related topics
—08	History and description with respect to kinds of persons
—09	Historical, geographic, persons treatment

More than one 0 is often used for a standard subdivision such as —03, —00.3, or —0003. The number of 0s used in a standard subdivision will vary to avoid conflicting with other numbers in the Schedule. If more than one 0 is required, there will always be appropriate instructions provided. Even though the standard subdivisions generally can be used with any number in the Schedules, it is always necessary to check the Schedules to see if there are special directions for a particular classification number, for example, the standard subdivision for Philosophy and theory, —01 :

200	Religion
200.1–.9	Standard subdivisions of religion
210	Philosophy and theory of religion

390	Customs, etiquette, folklore
390.001–.009	Standard subdivisions
.01–.09	Standard subdivisions of customs
.1–.4	Customs of specific economic, social, occupational classes

The standard subdivisions provide possibilities for further division within each subdivision. For example, standard subdivision —01 furnishes the following more specialized subdivisions:

—01	Philosophy and theory
—011	Systems
—012	Classification
—013	Value
—014	Language and communication
—015	Scientific principles
—(016)	Optional number for Bibliographies, catalogs, indexes
—019	Psychological principles

Table 2. Geographic Areas, Historical Periods, Persons

The notations in this Table, the largest one, allow a number to be expanded to indicate a geographical significance. Throughout the DDC Schedules, there are instructions to add from Table 2 to build a more specific classification number. Where no specific instructions are given *in* the Schedules for adding the area notation, the standard subdivision —09, for Historical, geographic, persons treatment, can be added to the base number, and then the area notation added to —09. Following is a summary of the Table.

—1	Areas, regions, places in general
—2	Persons
—3	The ancient world
—4	Europe Western Europe
—5	Asia Orient Far East
—6	Africa
—7	North America
—8	South America
—9	Other parts of the world and extraterrestrial worlds Pacific Ocean islands

The area notation —1 is used for areas not limited by continents, countries, or localities. Included are the treatment of a subject by region, areas, places, and groups in general. Also included here are such geographical features as frigid zones, landforms, oceans, and socioeconomic regions. Area notation —2 is used for biographical materials.

Conclusion

Through these devices, classifications are possible for an infinite number of subjects. By using adds and options, it is possible to make the notation as specific as practicable. However, many of the numbers will be too long for many small libraries. Libraries with smaller collections have a built-in option. Segmenting of DDC numbers is shown by spaces between digits in numbers; DDC numbers can be divided at these places without losing their meaning. Those that appear in one segment should generally be used without this reduction.

Literature Cited

Bloomberg, Marty, and Hans Weber. 1976. *An introduction to classification and number building in Dewey.* Ed. John Phillip Immroth. Littleton, CO: Libraries Unlimited.

Merrill, William Stetson. 1939. *Code for classifiers: Principles governing the consistent placing of books in a system of classification.* 2d ed. Chicago: American Library Association.

▐▐▌▌▌ 4

The Tables

Introduction

The seven Tables of DDC faceting (establishing aspects of subjects) were introduced in Edition 18, although a predecessor to Table 1 was found in the first edition. It was nicknamed "Form divisions," despite the fact that several features were in no way expressive of physical format, but eventually the obvious misnomer was dropped. Other precursors of the modern Tables appeared and disappeared abruptly. Edition 2 (1885) included three new ones called "Geographical divisions," which were little more than lists of topics that could be subdivided by region and used the history numbers in 930–999; two more gave pattern lists of class numbers and subject divisions for the various languages identified in the 400 class. Edition 13 (1932) introduced a fifth, which subdivided literatures in the 800 class. All of these auxiliary aids lasted until the so-called Standard Edition 15 dropped everything except a brief introduction to a method of subdividing, "where consideration of the form or style in which the book is written, as well as the subject, is important" (Dewey 1951, xiii).

Edition 16 restored the form divisions in a separate list similar to today's Table 1. The old "Geographic Table" appeared as a sequence of numbers "accompanied by instructions in the Schedules to 'divide like 930–999,' or 'like 940–999'" (Dewey 1958, 2:2421). Edition 17 renamed the "Form divisions" and restructured the Geographic Table into an "Area Table" with all the characteristics of the present Table 2. Edition 18 reactivated the discontinued Tables 3, 4, and 6 for language and literature. It also added two more: Table 5 for racial, ethnic, and national groupings and Table 7 for differentiating groups of persons.

Table 2 is by far the longest, occupying 371 pages (7 more than Edition 20), as contrasted with 31 pages for Table 1 (11 more than last edition), 31 for Table 3 (5 more), 7 for Table 4 (1 more), 20 for Table 5 (3 more), 26 for Table 6 (9 more), and 27 for Table 7 (3 more).

Some writers urge that "the principle of separate tables for certain subjects ought to be extended in future editions" (Croghan 1972, 74:120–21), much like the Add Tables found in many of the classes. This would mean Add instructions for using notations from other parts of the Schedule and making almost no use of these Tables except for a rare reference to Table 2 for a location. DDC editors seem more concerned with refining and expanding the existing Tables. They are also aware that faceting inevitably tempts classifiers to use close classification to the limits of its practicability. Witness the excessively long DDC numbers often found in Library of Congress records. They may be justified for indexing uses, such as the Universal Decimal Classification (UDC) was designed for, but they are usually more bother than help at the shelves.

Table 1. Standard Subdivisions

From the first, Melvil Dewey applied a rudimentary pattern for "mode of treatment" subdivisions. Edition 2 gave it a fixed form, reflecting to some extent notable features built into the Schedule proper. The morphology of Table 1 has changed little over intervening years, although extensive expansions and several significant alterations took place. Although the Summaries show no changes in a comparison of Table 1 of Editions 20 and 21, one can see that the Table is still evolving.

Schedule Manipulation of Table 1 Meanings

Table 1 facets may attach to class numbers of any length, for example:

403	Language dictionaries, encyclopedias, concordances
150.1	Philosophy and theory of psychology
581.072	Botanical research
614.43205	A serial publication on insects as disease carriers

It is the only fully generalized faceting device offered in *DDC*, the only table by which class numbers may be subdivided without specific schedule instructions. Conversely, it is subject to special instructions. Sometimes applying it is flatly forbidden. Elsewhere it is conceptually or notationally distorted, for example:

508   **Natural history**

        Do not use for history and description of natural sciences and mathematics with respect to groups of persons; class in 500.8

Sometimes part of the Table 1 meanings and notation are repeated in the schedule under a particular class number. Prima facie this practice seems redundant, but closer examination shows that in every case certain *ss* meanings are expanded, negated, or superseded.

Standard subdivision —04 (Special topics) is designed for local schedule manipulation. In Table 1 it carries a note to use only when "specifically set forth in the schedules."

We have observed that faceting, or number building, often poses citation order problems. Dewey's interposition of the 0 in front of his "form divisions" was to ensure their physical precedence over all other subdivisions of general class numbers. By *DDC 14* (published in 1942), a variety of other subdivision categories were often needed to section a broad topic adequately. Variation in the number of intervening zeros was the solution. Standard subdivision notation,

Table 1. Standard Subdivisions / 37

which normally does not involve a hierarchical structure because it is designed to be universally applicable, must be adjusted to provide normal citation order. The double zero is the commonest way to achieve this. More complicated situations require a third zero when the second one is, or may be, preempted.

A good example of the increasing generality of content that multiple zeros reflect can be seen in the summary for the history of Central Europe Germany. The fewer the zeros the more particular the content of the number. The most particular places have no zeros at all (e.g., Poland and Hungary).

943.000 1–.000 9	**Standard subdivisions of central Europe**
.001–.009	**Standard subdivisions of Germany**
.01–.08	**Historical periods of Germany**
.1	**Northeastern Germany**
.6	**Austria and Liechtenstein**
.7	**Czech Republic and Slovakia**
.8	**Poland**
.9	**Hungary**

DDC places a virtual taboo on adding one standard subdivision to another in the same number unless there are specific instructions to do so. Classifiers may find themselves in a quandary when more than one applies to the same work. There are instructions at the beginning of Table 1, a table of preference that indicates the citation order for Table 1.

Special topics	—04
Persons	—092
Auxiliary techniques and procedures; apparatus, equipment, materials	—028
(*except* —0288)	
Drafting illustrations	—0221
Education, research, related topics	—07
(*except* —074, —075, —076, —077)	
Management	—068
(Etc.)	

A restriction on free use of standard subdivisions affects works on topics that do not approximate the whole, that is, constitute not quite all but the greater part of the class at which it is located. Such topics are found in "including," "contains," "example," and "common name" notes. How to determine whether a topic approximates the whole of the contents of a number is discussed at length in the Manual.

Although there is no general auxiliary table for time divisions, Tables 1, 2, and 3 are frequently associated with temporal concepts. Standard subdivisions —0901–0905 (Historical periods) are a comprehensive span of time period numbers. Unless the Schedule gives a specific chronology, these numbers may be applied, like any Table 1 aspect, without instructions. Classes 800 and 900 contain many local chronologies. Internal Period Tables are frequently used with auxiliary Tables to build class numbers where time is a significant, but not the only, facet.

Table 1 *DDC 21* Revisions

The editors have expanded Table 1 by establishing a variety of new numbers that add depth and consistency to class numbers. Also in their effort to "ensure sensitivity," they have expanded persons with special social status (—0869) with new subdivisions to give more precise notations to various social groups. A list of examples (with indentations showing expansions) follows:

—086 91	Persons with status defined by changes in residence
—086 92	Antisocial and asocial persons
—086 923	Juvenile delinquents and predelinquents
—086 927	Offenders
—086 93	Nondominant groups
—086 94	Socially disadvantaged persons
—086 941	Unemployed persons
—086 942	The poor
—086 945	Abandoned children, abused children, children born out of wedlock, orphans
—086 947	Unmarried mothers
—086 949	Victims of war and crime
—086 96	Retired persons
—086 97	Veterans of military service

Other changes follow:

—019   Psychology of learning specific subjects (also 071) is now located here.

—021   Comprehensive works on Tables (—0212) now use this notation.

—0212   Formulas and specifications in specific times and places (—09) were moved here.

—024   Works for persons in specific occupations in specific times and places (—09) are now found here.

—0284   Apparatus, equipment, materials is a new number.

—0286   Waste technology is a new number.

—0601–09 Greek-letter societies (371.854) and student organizations (371.84) are now located here.

—071   Schools and courses became Education; curricula directed toward specific subject objectives (375.008) and curricula in specific subjects (375.01–.9) are now found here.

—0711   Curricula directed toward specific subject objectives in higher education (378.1992–.1998) are now here under Higher education.

Table 1. Standard Subdivisions / 39

—0712   Curricula directed toward specific subject objectives in secondary education (373.192–.198) are now under Secondary education.

—0715   Institutes and workshops, radio and television classes, correspondence courses (—07152–07154) now are found here.

—0727   Statistical methods used in specific kinds of research (—0722–0724) are now found here under Statistical methods, a new number.

—0728   Presentation of statistical data is a new number.

—0785   Computer-assisted instruction is a new number.

—08   History and description with respect to kinds of persons has a new table and now includes subject for persons with various nonoccupational characteristics (—02403–02408).

—08341   Boys six to eleven is a new number.

—08342   Girls six to eleven is a new number.

—0842   Comprehensive works on young adults (—0835) are now found here.

—08421   Young men is a new number.

—08422   Young women is a new number.

—086942   Vagrants (—08692) is now found here with The poor.

—089   Comprehensive works on nondominant racial, ethnic, national groups (—08693) are now found here under Racial, ethnic, national groups.

—09005   Serial publications under Historical, geographic, persons treatment is a new number.

—091   Maintenance and repair in areas, regions, places in general is found here and —028 is added. In specific continents, countries, localities is now —093–099 (—0288) plus —028 notation.

—0923   Collected persons treatment of members of specific racial, ethnic, national groups (—0922) is a new number.

—0929   Persons treatment of nonhumans, such as a biography of Lassie, is a new number.

Table 2. Geographic Areas, Historical Periods, Persons

Geographic or political subdivision was long dependent on the history divisions 930–990. Not only were subdivisions of 910 (Geography and travel) drawn from that span, but regional division in any discipline was based on Divide-like instructions referring to those numbers for patterns. As time went on, two problems emerged. First, the WASP bias from which the DDC still struggles to extricate itself dominated the history schedule, stressing political units, especially in Europe and the United States, over physical and other regional areas, that had to be spelled out as they were needed. Second, the Divide-like instructions were hard to follow. *DDC 17* initiated the now-familiar Area Table, with a section for regions and places in general. Other parts of the table expanded jurisdictional sequences, expanding those for Asia, Africa, and Oceania particularly. Although it retained its Divide-likes to cite other schedule spans, that edition referred to its auxiliary tables by means of Add notes. Divide-likes gave way entirely in *DDC 18* to "Add tos" (from schedule spans) and "Add froms" (for Tables).

The demarcation between areas —3 and —4–9 is not always so clear as could be wished, especially in view of the note under —3 to "class a specific part of ancient world not provided for here in —4–9" (v. 1, p. 27). A British classifier offered some advice:

> Under —3 "The Ancient world" are gathered those parts of the world more or less known *to* classical antiquity, and considered only during the period of "ancient history." The same areas in later times, as well as other areas such as America in both ancient and later times, are classed in —4–9 ... (Trotter 1980, 4).

Many class numbers can be geographically divided, without specific instructions by going first to Table 1. The *ss* —093–099 span (Treatment by specific continents, etc.) is most frequently used, but twenty other Table 1 entries say to add notation from Table 2.

The discussion of standard subdivisions noted that two are not used in the same number except when so instructed. One of the most frequent exceptions is for catalogs of exhibits (with geographical facets) housed in museums (also characterized by geographical facets).

In order to simplify instructions in the Schedules where standard subdivision 09 has been displaced from its regular position to the position of a legitimate subdivision of a class—namely, to 9, historical periods have been added to Table 2. They are still found in full in Table 1.

Table 2. Geographic Areas, Historical Periods, Persons / 41

Persons (as individuals or as individual members of a class of people) have been indicated by means of either Table 1 or 2 for quite a while. One has to be careful when determining which of the tables is the correct one to use in any particular instance. For example, elementary school teachers is 372.92, not 372.092.

Standard subdivisions —0924 for individual persons and —0926 for case histories are gone from Table 1 as well as from Table 2. In Table 2 the categories had been —24 and —26.

At the beginning of Table 2 and at area —4 are found the first instances of the two-level summary.

—1	**Areas, regions, places in general**
—2	**Persons**
—3	**The ancient world**
—4	**Europe Western Europe**
—5	**Asia Orient Far East**
—6	**Africa**
—7	**North America**
—8	**South America**
—9	**Other parts of world and extraterrestrial worlds Pacific Ocean islands**

Table 2 *DDC 21* Revisions

The reconfiguring of Europe following the demise of the Soviet Union has resulted in significant changes in Table 2. Eastern Europe and Russia (—47) were affected to such an extent that separate Tables were constructed to assist the user in following these changes. The Comparative Table is organized by country, and the Equivalence Table is by notation number; so, either way classifiers seek the information, it is readily available. Both Tables are found in the back of Volume I.

Besides these changes following the breakup of the Soviet states, other parts of Table 2 have also received attention. Norway has been extensively expanded, and Greece and Brazil have been revised. Jordan (which now includes the West Bank), Nigeria, and Haiti have been revised and expanded. All places in —93 were moved to make room for New Zealand to be expanded. There are now 6½ pages of new numbers for New Zealand in —93 to —9399, but only a few changes are included here.

At last it has been recognized that despite the Turkish invasion in the early 1970s, Cyprus remains an independent state because of its large Greek population. Thus, it has been moved from —5645, under Turkey, to —569, with Syria, Lebanon, Israel, and Jordan.

The Panama Canal, strangely enough, had been included under the Southeast Pacific Ocean (—1641). Now the editors recognize that it is more land than water and have placed it at —72875, under Panama. Can the Suez Canal be far behind? To make room for Bulgaria to move from its previous location (—4977), Skyros Island (—49515), Northern Sporades (—4954), Thasos Island (—4957), Comprehensive works on the Aegean Islands (—4958), and the Crete region (—4959) have been moved from —499.

In considering the massive transformations in the European regions since Edition 20, the editors should be applauded in the intelligent and logical ways that Schedule relocations have been accomplished.

Other changes follow:

—172   Socioeconomic regions by degree of economic development (—1723) is now found here.

Under Norway:

—4821   Oslo county (fylke) (—4823) is now here.

—4822   Akershus county (fylke) is a new number.

—4824   Hedmark county (fylke) is a new number.

—4825   Oppland county (fylke) is a new number.

—4826   Buskerud county (fylke) is a new number.

—4827   Vestfold county (fylke) is a new number.

—4828   Telemark county (fylke) is a new number.

—4831   Aust-Agder county (fylke) (—482) is now found here.

—4832   Vest-Agder county (fylke) (—482) is now found here.

—4833   Vestlandet is a new number.

—4834   Rogaland county (fylke) is a new number.

—4836   Hordaland county (fylke) is a new number.

—4838   Sogn og Fjordane county (fylke) is a new number.

—4839   Møre og Romsdal county (fylke) is a new number.

—4841   Sør-Trøndelag county (fylke) is a new number.

—4842   Nord-Trøndelag county (fylke) is a new number.

—4843   Comprehensive works on Northern Norway, or Nord-Nerge (—4845), are now found here.

—4844   Nordland county (fylke) (—4845) is now found here.

—4846   Finnmark county (fylke) (—4845) is now at this number.

Under Denmark:

—48914   Copenhagen county (—48913) has been moved here.

Under Greece:

—49515   Skyros Island (—499) has been consolidated here under Central Greece region.

—4954   Northern Sporades (—499) is now classed here under Thessaly region.

Table 2. Geographic Areas, Historical Periods, Persons / 43

—4957 Drama, Kavala nomes (—4956), and Thasos Island (—499) are now found here under Eastern Macedonia and the Thrace region.

—4958 Comprehensive works on the Aegean Islands (—499) are now found here.

—4959 The Crete region (—4998) is now located here.

Under Bulgaria:

—499 Bulgaria was moved from —4977.

Under China:

—5129 Hainan Province (—5127) is now found here.

Under Iran:

—5527 Markazi Province under Iran (—5525) has been relocated here.

Under Middle East:

—5693 Cyprus (—5645) is now found here.

Under Jordan:

—5695 West Bank is found under Jordan at —56951–56953.

—569567 Ṭafīlah Province is a new number.

—56957 Ma'ān Province is a new number; also, the eastern part of former Karak district (—56956) is now found here.

—56959 Zarqā' and Mafraq provinces is a new number; also, the eastern part of former Irbid district and Syrian Desert in Jordan (—56954) and northeastern part of former Amman district (—56958) are now located here.

—569593 Zarqā' Province

—569597 Mafraq Province

Under Nigeria:

—66926 Osun State (—66925) is now found here.

—66928 Ondo State is a new number.

—66932 Edo State is a new number.

—66936 Delta State is a new number.

—66943 Akwa Ibom State (—66944) is now found here.

—66945 Abia State (—66946) is now found here.

—66949 Enugu State (—66948) has been moved here.

—66956 The eastern part of former Kwara State (—66957) and the western part of former Benue State (—66954) are included here under Kogi State.

—66963 Kebbi State (—66962) is now found here.

—66976   Katsina State (—66973) has been moved here.

—66977   Jigawa State (—66978) has been relocated here.

—66987   Yobe State (—66985) is now found here.

—66989   Taraba State (—66988) has been relocated here.

Under Canada:

—71133   Langley (—71137) is now found here under Greater Vancouver Regional District.

—71334   St. Thomas (—71335) is now included under Elgin County.

—71336   Haldimand County (—71337) is now found here under Regional Municipality of Haldimand-Norfolk.

—71338   Lincoln County (—71351) is now located here under Regional Municipality of Niagara.

—71345   Waterloo City (—71344) is now found here under Kitchener-Waterloo.

—71347   Brantford (—71348) is now included here under Brant County.

—71356   Ontario County (—71355) was moved here under Regional Municipality of Durham.

—71367   Peterborough (—71368) is now found here under Peterborough County.

—71373   Grenville County (—71374) is now found here under United Counties of Leeds and Grenville.

—71375   Glengarry County (—71377) and Stormont County (—71376) are now found here under United Counties of Stormont, Dundas, and Glengarry.

—71385   Prescott County (—71386) was moved here under United Counties of Prescott and Russell.

Under Panama:

—72875   Panama Canal (—1641) is now found here under Canal Area.

Under Dominican Republic:

—729377   Monte Plata (—729374) is now found here.

—729381   Hato Mayor (—729384) has been moved here.

Under Haiti:

—72943   Nord and Nord-Est départements was only Nord département.

—729432   Nord département is a new number.

—729436   Nord-Est département is a new number.

Table 2. Geographic Areas, Historical Periods, Persons / 45

—729442 Centre département is a new number; also, Ouest département (—72945) and Nord département (—72943) are now found here under Centre département.

—729446 Artibonite département is a new number.

—72945 Ouest and Sud-Est départements were only Ouest département.

—729452 Ouest département is a new number.

—729456 Sud-Est département is a new number.

—72946 Sud and Grand' Anse départements were just Sud département.

—729462 Sud département is a new number.

—729466 Grand' Anse département is a new number.

Under Brazil:

—8111 Rondônia state (—8175) has been moved here.

—8117 Tocantins state (—8173) is now located here.

—8134 Fernando de Noronha Archipelago state (—8136) has been moved here.

Under Peru:

—8544 Loreto (—8543) is now found here.

Under Colombia:

—86166 Guaviare (—86165) has been moved here.

Under New Zealand:

—93 Comprehensive works on specific islands (—931) are now located here.

—931 North Island (—9312) is now found here.

—9312 Former Auckland Province (—93122) has been moved here.

—9346 Former Hawkes Bay Province (—93125) is now found here under Hawke's Bay Region.

—9348 Former Taranaki Province (—93123) is now classed here under Taranaki Region.

—936 Former Wellington Province (—93127) is now found here under Wellington Region.

—937 South Island (—9315) is now located here.

—9396 Stewart Island (—931575) is now located here under Southland District.

—9399 Outlying islands (—9311) has been moved here.

Under Solomon Islands:

—95936   Isabel Province (—95935) is now found here.

—95938   Makira and Ulawa Province (—95939) is now located here.

—9712   South Georgia and South Sandwich Islands (—9711) are now found here.

—989   British Antarctic Territory (—9711) is now found here under Antarctica.

Table 3. Subdivisions for the Arts, for Individual Literatures, for Specific Literary Forms

The third Table is for application with 700.4, 791.4, and 808–809, according to instructions. It is divided into three parts:

A: description, critical appraisal, biography, single or collected works of an individual author

B: for two or more authors and rhetoric in specific literary forms

C: additional elements used in number building within Table 3B

Use of the Tables may be difficult for novices, so assistance is provided for 3A in four-step instructions; 3B and 3C have eight steps for application each. In addition, flowcharts are available in the Manual to assist classifiers in using the Tables.

Table 3 *DDC 21* Revisions

Alterations in Table 3 are few, but one is fairly significant. In 3C, Arts and literature dealing with specific themes and subjects (—3) has been expanded and modified for application with 700.4.

Other changes in Edition 21 follow:

Table 3B

—2   Miscellaneous drama (—2057) is now found here.

Table 3C

—1   Arts and literature displaying specific qualities of style, mood, viewpoint has been expanded with new numbers under —11 and —16.

—93–99   Literature for and by persons of racial, ethnic, national groups in continents, countries, and localities where the groups predominate (—8) was moved here.

Table 6. Languages / 47

Table 4. Subdivisions of Individual Languages and Language Families

Table 3 is for application with literatures, and Table 4 is for use with 400 Language and language families.

Table 4 *DDC 21* Revisions

There was one change in the fourth Table:

—81   Spellers (—31) has been consolidated here under Words.

Table 5. Racial, Ethnic, National Groups

The fifth Table includes Racial, Ethnic, National Groups, which may be used with —089 from Table 1 or directly applied to numbers where directed.

Table 5 *DDC 21* Revisions

A new number, —9594, has been developed under East and Southeast Asian peoples; Mundas for Miao (Hmong) and Yao peoples. Also, the editors created new subdivisions under Other Iranian peoples (—9159): for Kurds (—91597) and Baluchi (—91598).

Other changes in Edition 21 follow:

—9149   Nuri (—91499) is now included here under Other Indic peoples.

—9157   Tajik (—9159) is now found here.

—9186   Moravians (—9187) has been moved here.

—92   Chaldeans (—921) is now found here under Semites.

—9279   Maltese (—9277) has been moved here.

Table 6. Languages

While most libraries using DDC seldom need to subdivide by language, it is a facet that should be recognized in any fully developed classification scheme. For instance, certain classic works are held in a variety of translations by special libraries, or in comprehensive collections. Table 6 stems from class 400, although it warns that its notation does not necessarily correspond to the schedule spans 420–490 and 810–890. Uses of Table 6 are illustrated by the following examples:

```
305.721052 English-speaking people of Japan
305          Social groups
  .7            Language groups
  .72            English and Old English (Anglo-Saxon)
  .721             English
  .7210             [geographic indicator]
  .72105              Asia
  .721052              Japan

897.5      Cherokee literature
897          Literatures of North American native languages
  .5            Cherokee [from —975 in Table 6]
```

Table 6 *DDC 21* Revisions

A lot of work has been done on Table 6, with many categories expanded. Examples are Turkic (—943), Niger-Congo (—963), North American native (—97), Polynesian languages (—994), Caucasian (Caucasic) languages (—999), and Quechan (Kechuan), Aymaran, Tucanoan, Tupi, Arawaken (—983).

Other changes follow:

—39   Comprehensive works on Old Low Germanic languages (—391) were relocated here.

—391   Yiddish (—37) is now found here under Other Germanic languages.

—392   Old Frisian (—391) is now found here with Frisian.

—3931   Old Low Franconian (—391) is now found here under Dutch.

—394   Old Low German and Old Saxon (—391) are now located here under Low German (Plattdeutsch).

—491   Langue d'oc (—41) is now classed here under Provençal.

—9149   Nuristani, Kafiri (—91499), is now located here.

—91497   Romany (—91499) was moved here.

—9156   Dari (—9155) is now found here.

—9157   Tajik (—9159) has been moved here.

—9159   Pamir languages (—91593) is now located here.

—9186   Moravian dialects (—9187) is now located here under Czech.

—928   Argobba (—9287) has been relocated here.

—9511   Beijing dialect (—9517) is now found here under Mandarin.

—954   Himalayan languages, other than Kiranti languages and Newari (—9549), are now found here.

—963977 Ndebele, South Africa (—96398), is now located here under Sotho-Tswana group.

Table 7. Groups of Persons / 49

—98   Yaruro (—983) was moved here.

—98324   Aymaran languages (—98323) were relocated here.

Table 7. Groups of Persons

Table 7 may be used according to instructions at specific schedule locations, or in other tables. Examples follow:

741.9088616   A collection of drawings made by physicians
741   Drawing and drawings
  .9   Collections of drawings
  .908   History and description with respect to kinds of persons
              [—08 from Table 1]

  .9088   Occupational and religious groups
              —00809–08899 Specific occupational and religious groups
              Add to base number —088 notation 09–99 from Table 7
  .09886   Persons occupied with applied sciences [—6 from Table 7]
  .098861   Persons occupied with medical sciences
  .0988616   With specific medical specialties

Table 7 *DDC 21* Revisions

—03   Comprehensive works on members of nondominant racial,
           ethnic, national groups (—0693) were moved here.

—0562   Comprehensive works on young adults (—055) are now found
           here under Young adults.

—2   Comprehensive works on members of nondominant religious
           groups (—0693) were moved here.

—2999   Theosophy (—291) is now classed here with Religions of other origin.

—309   Educational sociologists (—37) is now found here under
           Persons occupied with sociology and anthropology.

—351   Heads of local governments (—354) and Specific kinds of
           heads of governments (—3511 through —3518) are now found
           here under Heads of government and their deputies.

—352   Administrators and commissioners (—3523) are now found here
           under Other government personnel.

—3527   Local government workers (—354) are now located here under
           Civil service personnel.

—55   Oceanography (—553) is now found here under Persons
           occupied with earth sciences.

—57   Comprehensive works on biology (—574) are now found here
           under Persons occupied with life sciences.

—577   Ecology (—574) is now found here.

—579 Microbiology (—574), fungi and algae (—58), Bacteriology (—589), and Protozoology (—593) are now consolidated here under Microbiology.

—599 Physical ethnology (—572) and Physical anthropology (—573) are now found here.

—63 Farming (—631) is now located here under Persons occupied with agriculture and related technologies.

—792 Drama (—7921) is now found here under Stage presentations.

Literature Cited

Croghan, Antony. 1972. The Dewey Decimal Classification and its eighteenth edition. *Library Association Record* 74 (7): 120–21.

Dewey, Melvil. 1951. *Decimal Classification.* 15th ed. Lake Placid Club, NY: Forest Press.

————. 1958. *Dewey Decimal Classification and Relative Index.* 16th ed. Vol. 2. Lake Placid Club, NY: Forest Press.

Trotter, Ross. 1980. Dewey 19—A subjective assessment. *Catalogue & Index* 59: 4.

Class 000
Generalities

Introduction

This class bore no name in Dewey's first edition (1876), but it has long been called the "General works" or "Generalia" class. As indicated by its name, it is a mixture of related and only vaguely related subjects, the least of which is Library and information sciences (020). But it also contains News media, journalism, publishing (070), Knowledge (001), The book (002), Systems (003) (not to be confused with computer systems), Data processing Computer science (004), Computer programming, programs, data (005), and lastly, Special computer methods (006). Some have doubts about this mixture, such as Bloomberg and Weber (1976, 43), who remarked that 070, News media, journalism, publishing, might better be located with the disciplinary material in sections for specific kinds of communication, such as postal and telecommunications (383–384).

Outline and Details of Class 000

000	Generalities
010	Bibliography
020	Library and information sciences
030	General encyclopedic works
040	[Unused]
050	General serial publications
060	General organizations and museology
070	News media, journalism, publishing
080	General collections
090	Manuscripts and rare books

Division 000:   In the first subdivision of the schedules the true "generalities" of the class reside, including broad, fundamental concepts of learning, culture, and research as well as disputable or questionable information such as UFOs (001). The second section contains general concepts and interdisciplinary pieces about monographs (002), followed by general concepts of prediction, computerized representations, intercourse, and information, and theories of making decisions (003). Needing a good home, the topics of data processing and computer science found this a welcoming place with plenty of room to grow and one that eliminates the need to decide the argument of whether computers should be considered more science than technology, or whether the machines should be placed with their applications (004–006).

Division 010:   The next division is reserved for bibliographies or lists of titles that may appear in any format or a particular format, on a particular subject, or from a particular place (010–016). Also found here are such lists as specific collections or catalogs, including the catalogs of libraries (017–019).

Division 020:   The third division in the schedules contains all information involving libraries and related disciplines (020–027) and one section on the use of informational materials and reading as an activity (028).

Division 030:   Encyclopedias that include information on broadly diverse topics are found in the fourth division. The first section is for books of general facts and standard subdivisions of the division (030), followed by encyclopedias organized by language (031–039).

Division 040:   Unused in this edition.

Division 050:   All publications that are periodically issued are found in this division and are arranged like 030 with general publications and standard subdivisions for the division first (050) followed by works organized by language (051–059).

Division 060:   Organizations that are not related to a specific field or discipline are located in this division with an arrangement similar to 030 and 050 with general organizations and standard subdivisions of the division first (060), then works arranged by country (061–068). Museums, because they are considered general organizations, or perhaps because there was no other logical place to put them, conclude the division (069).

Division 070:   Journalism in all forms, including newspapers, periodicals, motion pictures, and broadcast media, is in this division. It is organized like the previous three divisions with general aspects (070.1–.4) and standard subdivisions (070.01–.09) for the division first (070), then the remaining sections are arranged by location (071–079). Historical and persons treatment of journalism and newspapers (070.9) are found separate from this geographic treatment. All aspects of publishing, including book publishing, are also included in the first section (070.5). The Historical, geographic, persons treatment of publishing (070.509) is separated from that of journalism.

Division 080: As in the preceding divisions, collections of addresses, lectures, essays, interviews, graffiti, and quotations in general and the standard subdivisions for the division are first (080) and such collections grouped by language follow (081–089). Works that emphasize the literary form and quality of these formats are not included in this division but are placed with literature.

Division 090: Manuscripts (091) and rare materials or works that are unusual for some reason, such as through their ownership or origin, and titles that are forgeries or hoaxes are in the concluding sections of the first class of the schedules (092–099).

The Number Building Process

Example 1. A bibliography of Chinese legal literature in English.

A review of the division summations above indicates that bibliographies are found in 011–019, with bibliographies and catalogs of works from specific places found in 015. However, this work is *about* Chinese legal literature *but not written in Chinese.* Looking further, 016 is Bibliographies and catalogs of works on specific subjects or in specific disciplines, in this case, legal subject matter.

016

Looking under 016 we find "Add to base number 016 notation 001–999" and "Add to the various subdivisions of 016 notation 01–09 from Table 1 as required." Reviewing the summaries found at the front of Volume 2, the "Hundred Divisions" show law is found in 340, and the "Thousand Section" indicate Law of specific jurisdictions and areas is found in 349.

016.349

Under 349 in the Schedule we find:

> **.1** **Law of specific socioeconomic regions**
> Add to base number 349.1 the numbers following —17 in notation 171–177 from Table 2 ...
>
> **.4–.9** **Laws of specific jurisdictions and areas of modern world**
> Add to base number 349 notation 4–9 from Table 2 ...

Looking in the Table 2 Summary, Asia is found at —5, and China at —51.

016.34951 *Chinese Law, Past and Present: A Bibliography of Enactments and Commentaries in English Text.*

Example 2.   A work on computer use training.

The Relative Index has no listings for *computer training;* however, computers are found in 004.

004

The Summary for 004 follows:

004.01–.09	**Standard subdivisions**
.1	**General works on specific types of computers**
.2	**Systems analysis and design, computer architecture, performance, evaluation**
.3	**Processing modes**
.5	**Storage**
.6	**Interfacing and communications**
.7	**Peripherals**
.9	**Nonelectronic data processing**

The work would seem to fall in either 004 or 004.1, depending on whether it is about training in computer use in general or for a specific type of computer. Reviewing the piece more closely, we find that it is about microcomputer, or PC, training.

004.1

Looking under 004.1 in the Schedule, we find these choices:

.11	Digital supercomputers
.12	Digital mainframe computers
.14	Digital minicomputers
.16	Digital microcomputers
	Class here laptop, notebook, palmtop, pen, personal, pocket computers: personal digital assistants, workstations, comprehensive works on minicomputers and microcomputers.
	See Manual at 004.11–004.16
.19	Hybrid and analog computers

The "See Manual" reference at 004.11–004.16 instruction directs the classifier as follows:

Use these numbers and the analogous engineering numbers (621.3911–.3916) with caution: use them only for works that emphasize the specific type of computer, not for works that may refer most of the time to a particular type as an illustration of what computers in general do.

Clearly, this work is about microcomputer training specifically, and so we feel more confident of this number.

004.16

Now for training, we refer to the standard subdivisions in Table 1. Training is related to Education, which is found at —07 with "research and related topics." The Summary at —07 indicates that education (training) is found at —071.

004.16071   *The Computer Training Handbook*

DDC 21 Revisions

DDC 21 has little change in the broad outline of the class. Because of its nature, Generalities has always tended to be fairly stable; yet being the home of Data processing Computer science, it will experience a greater number of changes as it and related technologies progress rapidly in the next century.

The Summaries of Editions 20 and 21 display only one minor change in the headings. Despite this small change, the class as a whole has undergone a great deal of evolutionary change, especially in Data processing Computer science.

Summary (*DDC 20*)		Summary (*DDC 21*)	
050	**General serials and their indexes**	**050**	**General serial publications**

Computers and related topics found their home at last in the areas of 004–006 with Edition 20. Data processing and computer science have wandered throughout the Schedules, appearing in 001.64 as late as Edition 19 and in various places in 600 in Edition 14. Computation instruments and machines were found at 510.78 in Edition 15, although other aspects remained in 651.26 and 621.34. Edition 16 split the topics among 510.78, 681.14, and 651.2. Edition 17 found the machines and their use scattered around the 600 main class of Technology, although 510.78 was retained for mathematics and comprehensive works. Edition 18 moved data processing (its general parts) to 001.6, but office applications remained at 651.8. These various aspects remained separated in Edition 19 with few changes.

By 1983, the editor pointed out the difficulties in this situation to the Decimal Classification Editorial Policy Committee (EPC), which quickly decided to put this problem in order. By 1985 the publication of *Dewey Decimal Classification: 004–006 Data Processing and Computer Science and Changes in Related Disciplines*, produced primarily by assistant editor Julianne Beall, was released with an enthusiastic response from users. However, even with this improvement, 651.8 continued to be used for office functions, and word processing was found in 652.5.

It is not surprising that data processing and computer science (004–006) have been revised and expanded, with many new numbers and "new special provisions for processing modes, operating systems, and user interfaces" (Dewey 1996, 1:xxv). The Relative Index indicates how computer topics are distributed.

Computer architecture	004.22
engineering	621.392
Computer communications	004.6
communications services	384.3
engineering	621.398 1
programming	005.711
programs	005.713
Computer control	629.89
Computer engineering	621.39

The topics are comfortably situated in 004–006, for software or users' aspects, and 621.39(+) for engineering and manufacturing. Applications, such as computer network resources (025.04) and statistical presentations (001.422 602 8566), are classed in the discipline of the application.

Within the Generalities class, Data processing Computer science (004) includes hardware (except for repair, which is in 621.39) *and* programs and data that relate directly to the hardware, such as interfacing and communications. The 005 class includes programming, programs, and data only; and special computer applications, such as artificial intelligence and computer graphics, are located in 006.

Recognizing the complexity of the subject, the editors provided extensive direction in the application of the Schedules, devoting nearly 20 full pages of the Manual to guidelines and examples. A series of "Key questions" provides pathways to the appropriate places in the Schedules. Sample titles, their class numbers, and the reasoning behind the class assignments should answer any final questions about how to class a computer science title.

As discussed above, an inventory of changes in the Generalities class shows that most activity occurred in computer science.

004	Interactive, online, real-time data processing, which involves immediate results (004.33), is now found here under Data processing Computer science.
004.019	Psychological principles was Human-computer interaction.
004.3	Processing modes now includes Multiprogramming or Multitasking (004.32).
004.338	Systems analysis and design, computer architecture, performance evaluation of real-time computers is a new number.
004.357	Specific multiprocessor computers is a new number.
004.358	Systems analysis and design, computer architecture, performance evaluation of multiprocessor computers is a new number. Comprehensive works on these subjects are now in 004.3581–.3584.
004.3585	Systems analysis and design, computer architecture, performance evaluation of specific multiprocessor computers is a new number.
004.5	Virtual memory (004.54) is now found here under Storage.
004.563	Magnetic disks is a new number.
004.565	Optical external storage is a new number.

004.678   The fast-growing method for computer-based communication, the Internet, has now found a unique number here under Data processing   Computer science. But class works about the Internet here only if they deal with a considerable amount of computer science in general and some computer hardware in particular. Otherwise, class items dealing with communications software in 005.713, with search and retrieval in 025.04, or in 384.33, for those dealing with the economics and policies of the Internet.

004.718   Peripherals for computers distinguished by processing modes is a new number.

004.719   Peripherals for hybrid and analog computers is a new number.

005.114   Functional programming is a new number.

005.115   Logic programming is a new number.

005.117   Object-oriented programming is a new number.

005.118   Visual programming is a new number.

005.2   Specific machine and assembly languages (005.136) are now found here under Programming for specific types of computers, etc.

005.268   Programming for specific operating systems is a new number.

005.269   Programming for specific user interfaces is a new number.

005.27   Programming for processing modes is a new number.

005.273   Programming for real-time computer systems is a new number.

005.275   Programming for multiprocessor computers is a new number.

005.276   Programming for distributed computer systems is a new number.

005.28   Programming for specific operating systems and for specific user interfaces is a new number.

005.282   Programming for specific operating systems is a new number.

005.284   Programming for specific user interfaces is a new number.

005.304   Special topics under Programs is a new number.

005.3042   Specific programs is a new number.

005.368   Programs for specific operating systems and for specific user interfaces is a new number under digital microcomputers.

005.3684   Programs for specific user interfaces is a new number.

005.422   Systems programming for specific types of computers, for specific operating systems, for specific user interfaces is a new number.

005.424	Process management programming is a new number.
005.425	Memory management programming is a new number.
005.426	File system management programming is a new number.
005.428	Programming of user interfaces is a new number.
005.432	Specific operating systems is a new number.
005.434	Comprehensive works on multiprogramming, or multitasking (004.32), are consolidated here with Process management programs, a new number.
005.435	Comprehensive works on virtual memory (004.54) were moved here under Memory management programs, a new number.
005.436	File system management programs is a new number.
005.437	User interfaces is a new number.
005.438	Specific user interfaces is a new number.
005.741	Sorting and merging (005.748) is now found here under File organization and access methods, a new number.
005.752	Flat-file databases is a new number.
005.7525	Specific flat-file database management systems is a new number.
005.757	Object-oriented databases is a new number.
005.7575	Specific object-oriented database management systems is a new number.
005.758	Distributed data files and databases is a new number.
005.759	Full-text database management systems is a new number.
005.7592	Hypertext databases is a new number.
005.7598	Specific full-text database management systems is a new number.
005.84	Computer viruses is a new number.
005.86	Data backup and recovery is a new number.
006.32	Perceptrons (006.42) is now found classed here with Neural nets or networks, a new number.
006.331	Knowledge acquisition is a new number.
006.332	Knowledge representation is a new number.
006.333	Deduction, problem solving, and reasoning is a new number.
006.336	Programming for knowledge-based systems is a new number.
006.3363	Programming languages for knowledge-based systems is a new number.

006.337   Programming for knowledge-based systems for specific types of computers, operating systems, and user interfaces is a new number.

006.338   Programs for knowledge-based systems is a new number.

006.425   Handwriting recognition is a new number.

006.663   Programming languages for computer graphics is a new number.

006.6633 Specific programming languages for computer graphics is a new number.

006.69   Special topics in computer graphics is a new number.

006.693   Three-dimensional graphics is a new number.

006.696   Computer animation is a new number.

006.7   This is a new number for Multimedia systems and Interactive video, which were moved from 006.6. Comprehensive works on computer graphics and computer sound synthesis also merged here from 006.6.

006.72   Hardware is a new number.

006.76   Programming for multimedia systems is a new number.

006.77   Multimedia systems programming for specific types of computers, operating systems, and user interfaces is a new number.

006.78   Programs for multimedia systems is a new number.

Other changes in this class were much less dramatic. Research and Statistical methods show some reductions and relocations.

001.422   Tabulation and analysis of data (001.4224–.4225) has been absorbed by Statistical methods.

001.433   The Collection of data (001.4222) in Research was consolidated here with Descriptive method.

Libraries for educational institutions finds consolidations for materials that are comprehensive works.

027.7   College and university libraries now includes comprehensive works on instructional materials centers (027.8 and 371.3078)

027.8   School libraries now also includes comprehensive works on school resource centers (371.3078).

Exercises in the Use of Class 000

The following exercises are given for practice in interpreting and assigning DDC numbers. The works have been selected from Library of Congress (LC) and other libraries to demonstrate the nature and relative quantity of DDC classification. The class numbers are assigned by these libraries, as are all examples in this work, and are not the author's responsibility. Using all Schedules, Tables, and methodologies discussed in previous chapters, assign class numbers, then check them against the numbers found in "Answers to the Exercises" in the appendix.

1. A work on how to assign DDC classification numbers.
2. A work on lists of American books that are available to purchase from the publishers.
3. A work on Home Pages and the World Wide Web.
4. A work on how to charge for electronic services.
5. A work on lists of British books that are available to purchase from the publishers.
6. A work on the steps involved in bringing up circulation systems.
7. A work on programming for Windows (computer application).
8. A work on software development.
9. A work on programming in Dylan (computer language).
10. A work on creating graphics programs for Windows (computer application).

Literature Cited

Bloomberg, Marty, and Hans Weber. 1976. *An introduction to classification and number building in Dewey*. Ed. John Phillip Immroth. Littleton, CO: Libraries Unlimited.

Dewey, Melvil. 1996. *Dewey Decimal Classification and Relative Index*. 21st ed. Vol. 1. Albany, NY: Forest Press.

Class 100
Philosophy, Paranormal
Phenomena, Psychology

Introduction

The traditional branches of philosophy are situated in divisions of the 100 class; however, Aesthetics is found under the division of metaphysics at 111.85.

Metaphysics	the study of the source and substance of reality (110)
Epistemology	the study of what one can know about reality (120)
Logic	the study of valid inference (160)
Ethics	the study of proper conduct (170)
Aesthetics	the study of beauty (111.85)

The specific philosophical schools are separated from the other elements of philosophy on one side by Paranormal phenomena (130) and the other by Psychology (150). Paranormal phenomena began in Edition 1 as Anthropology, then changed to Mind and body in Edition 2. Classed here were the manifestations of the physical world upon the mind, including the brain.

Psychology (150) was originally known as Mental faculties, which were completely separate from physical considerations. Aspects include what the mind does, such as think and feel, so Psychology appears to be situated in the proper place, amidst other subjects that deal with the mind.

Outline and Details of Class 100

100	Philosophy and psychology
110	Metaphysics
120	Epistemology, causation, humankind
130	Paranormal phenomena

140	Specific philosophical schools
150	Psychology
160	Logic
170	Ethics (Moral philosophy)
180	Ancient, medieval, Oriental philosophy
190	Modern western and other non-Oriental philosophy

Division 100: Only the standard subdivisions for philosophy in general are found in the first section (101–109).

Division 110: Metaphysics is found in the first of the branches of philosophy in the Schedules, and includes ontology (111); the character of the universe including the origin and nature of life, or cosmology (113); and physical concepts of the universe such as the correlation of space and matter (114); eternity, the relationship between time and motion (115); evolution, motion, and process (116); matter, form, order, and chaos (117); power and force (118); and concepts of quantity (119).

Division 120: This division also contains philosophical works. These include philosophical aspects of knowledge, faith, and values, or epistemology (121); chance, cause, purpose, and freedom of will (123–124). Also found in this division are features of the human race such as aspects of perception (126–127); and works on attributes of human life including emotions and human souls (128–129).

Division 130: The fourth division moves away from the discipline of philosophy and contains works on the supernatural and topics that are outside scientifically known phenomena. Themes found here include ways to achieve a successful life that are outside of natural law or are in the realm of the supernatural (131). However, these would be "secular phenomena" as opposed to that involved in a religious experience, which is found in 200. Next come ghosts and haunted places (133.1); various methods of fortune-telling (133.3); devil worship, witchcraft, and magic (133.4); astrology (133.5); palmistry (133.6); psychic phenomena (133.8); and spiritualism (133.9). Other such phenomena are nonpsychological aspects of dreams (135), and unusual methods of ascertaining character and mental abilities such as handwriting (137); analysis of physical features (138); and the skull (139).

Division 140: This division returns to the discipline of philosophy and contains specific schools and viewpoints. These include idealism and related topics (141); critical philosophy (142); Bergsonism and intuitionism (143); humanism and related topics (144); sensationalism (145); naturalism and related topics (146); pantheism and related topics (147); dogmatism, eclecticism, liberalism, syncretism, and traditionalism (148). Other philosophical schools, such as realism and mysticism conclude the division (149).

Division 150: The Schedules leave philosophy again in this division, which is used for the discipline of psychology. The first section contains only the standard subdivisions of psychology (150.1–.9). Aspects of psychology follow, such as sensation, movement, emotions, and drives (152); intellectual processes (153); and aspects of the conscious mind (054). Applications of psychology conclude the division. These are the study of growth and individualization (155); the psychological comparison of humans and other living organisms (156); and the application of psychology to effect individual improvement (158).

Division 160: This division, which contains logic, is short as pages go but is filled with ideas and theories. The important principles of induction (161) and deduction (162) lead off, followed by errors and fictions (165); syllogisms (166); hypotheses (167); controversy, debate, and influencing by reason (168); and ending with analogy (169).

Division 170: This division, used for ethics, returns to philosophy because ethics is the same as moral philosophy. The first section is used for standard subdivisions of ethics (170.1–.9), with the special topics of metaethics and normative ethics (170.4). Various systems of ethics are next (171), with the remaining section numbers used for the various categories of ethics. These are ethics involving the political state (172) followed by ethics within the family (173); ethics of work or professions (174); social activities, amusement, and entertainment (175); ethics involving procreation and other sexual activities (176); ethics involved in social relationships (177); the ethics of gluttony, greed, and the use of addictive substances (178); the treatment and respect for other life, foul speech, vices, and virtues (179) conclude the division.

Division 180: This division is used for ancient, medieval, and Oriental philosophy. The first section contains only the standard subdivisions for the division (180.01–.09), and for ancient philosophy (180.1–.9). Oriental philosophy follows (181) with the standard subdivisions of Oriental philosophy (181.001–.009) and philosophies based on specific religions (181.04–.09), followed by the philosophies of various geographical areas (181.1–.9). The ancient philosophies, including pre-Socratic (182), Sophistic, and Socratic philosophies (183), Platonic (184), Aristotelian (185), skeptic and neoplatonic (186), Epicurean (187), and stoic (188) come next. Medieval western philosophies conclude the division (189).

Division 190: The last division of the class is for post-Medieval western and all other philosophies arranged by geographic location (191–199).

The Number Building Process

Example 1.   A work on the psychological and anthropological aspects of the people of Fiji.

Analyzing the work, we find that it is about the psychological development of the individuals in Fiji. Looking in the Relative Index we find:

Development	
biology	571.8
economics	338.9
sociology	303.44
Developmental abnormalities	571.938
Developmental biology	571.8
humans	612.6
microorganisms	571.842 9
Developmental disabilities	571.938
Developmental genetics	571.85
Developmental immunology	571.963 8
Developmental linguistics	401.93
Developmental psychology	155

We find possibilities in 571.8 for physical and 155 for mental development. Under 571.8 we find notations .84 Reproduction and growth of cells, and .876 Development in distinct stages which examines development in micro to macro views. The material is about the *mental* development rather than *physical* development of children. Turning to mental development we find 155 is Differential and developmental psychology, which is right on target.

155

Now, how to get the racial or anthropological aspects of mental development? Checking under 155 we find the following facets or aspects listed in the summary:

.2	Individual psychology
.3	Sex psychology and psychology of the sexes
.4	Child psychology
.5	Psychology of young people twelve to twenty
.6	Psychology of adults
.7	Evolutional psychology
.8	Ethnopsychology and national psychology
.9	Environmental psychology

The obvious selection would be .8 to bring in the ethnic and national aspects of the subject.

155.8

Under 155.8 we find the following:

.81	Nonliterate peoples
.82	Racial and ethnic differences
.84	Specific racial and ethnic groups
.89	National psychology

The work is about a specific ethnic group (Fijian), so the next part of the call number is 155.84.

155.84

Under .84 we find the following:

Add to base number 155.84 notation 03–099 from Table 5 ...

In Table 5, Fijians are included in the "other" group in —9, where we find —995 for Fijians. Since this work is about Fijians in their homeland, no further notation is required.

155.84995   *Body, Self, and Society: The View from Fiji.*

Example 2   A work on European witchcraft in the fifteenth century.

The Relative Index indicates that witchcraft is found at 133.43. Turning to 133.43 in the Schedules, we find the following:

.43	Magic and witchcraft
	Standard subdivisions are added for either or both topics in heading.
.430 9	Historical, geographic, persons treatment
	Class here history of witch crazes

This work is definitely a Historical, geographic, persons treatment, and gauging by the era, "witch crazes" is quite appropriate.

133.4309

Now that we have designated the topic of witchcraft, the next task is to establish the place (Europe) and time (fifteenth to eighteenth centuries), but which comes first? Looking in the table of preference at the beginning of Table 1, we find Treatment by specific continents, countries, localities; extraterrestrial worlds (—093–099) comes before Historical periods (—0901–0905). So, we must first establish the number for the location. In Table 1 under —093 through —099, we find the following:

Add to base number 09 notation 3–9 from Table 2 ...

Turning to Table 2 (Areas, Periods, Persons), we find Europe is listed as —4.

133.43094

In Table 1 we find historical periods are —090 1–090 5, with the fifteenth century at —090 24.

133.4309409024   *Early Modern European Witchcraft (1400–1700)*

DDC 21 Revisions

There has been no change in the broad outline of class 100. Philosophy continues rather stable, with just a minor relocation from Logic to Epistemology, causation, humankind. Paranormal phenomena had a minor reduction, and Astrology (133.5) was expanded. There were also some minor shifts in Ethics (Moral philosophy) and Ancient, medieval, Oriental philosophy.

121.68   Reference (160) was moved here from Logic to join Semantics under Meaning, interpretation, and hermeneutics.

133.323   Telediesthesia (Distant prospection) (133.3239) was relocated here under Dowsing.

Expanded Astrology:

133.50882 History and description with respect to specific religious groups is a new number.

133.5089 History and description with respect to specific racial, ethnic, national groups is a new number.

133.509   Historical, geographic, persons treatment, and Treatment by specific continents, countries, localities, extraterrestrial worlds (133.5093–.5099) are also new numbers.

133.526   The first six signs of the zodiac are in .5262–.5267, new numbers.

133.527   The second six signs of the zodiac are in .5272–.5277, new numbers.

133.5304 Special topics include Houses (.53042) and Aspects (.53044), new numbers.

133.531   The planets, sun, moon, and asteroids are located in .531–.5398, new numbers.

133.59   Schools of astrology are found in .59–.594, new numbers.

Psychology continues to be the most dynamic part of the 100 class. Revisions in it began in Edition 17 (1965) and have continued, but at a slower pace. Dianetics (158.9) was moved from its former position in Systems and schools of applied psychology to Comparative and non-Christian religions under Scientology (299.936). With the relocation in Edition 20 of Abnormal and clinical psychology to Medicine (616.89), 150 does not encompass any diseased states or mental disorders, although Counseling and interviewing (158.3) is found under Applied psychology. Thus psychology encompasses the functions of the mind or brain, not the dysfunctions. Three of the changes listed below deal with psychology as it relates to specific groups of people (children and young adults).

152.182   Itch and tickle (152.1828) was moved here under Cutaneous (Tactile) perception.

155.456   Child psychology of the upper classes (155.4562) was relocated here under Children distinguished by social and economic levels, by level of cultural development.

155.4567   Migrant children (155.45675) is now found here under Socially and culturally disadvantaged children.

155.65   Comprehensive works on young adults (155.5) have been moved here under Young adults.

158   Cooperation under Applied psychology (158.5) is now located here under Applied psychology.

175   Ethics of specific types of recreation (175.1–.9) has been relocated here under Ethics of recreation, leisure, public performances, communication.

179.3   Ethics of hunting (175) was moved here under Treatment of animals.

180   The philosophy of ancient and medieval Greece (180.938) has been relocated here under Ancient, medieval, Oriental philosophy.

181.112   Confucian philosophy now includes interdisciplinary works on Confucianism (299.512).

Exercises in the Use of Class 100

Utilizing the following brief summaries, test your skills at number building; then, compare your classification with the class numbers found in "Answers to the Exercises" in the appendix.

1. A pop psychology work on a standard of ethics in daily living.
2. A work on how people in some occupations commercialize their feelings.
3. A work on Yoga.
4. A Freudian analysis of the situation of humanity after Eden.
5. A work on motivation and personal improvement through meditation.
6. A psychological study of a young Hungarian Jewish girl during World War II.

7

Class 200
Religion

Introduction

Criticisms of Dewey's personal religious biases and of the shortcomings of class 200 are not wanting. They arose early on, from most types of libraries and most faiths, e.g. Roman Catholicism, Christian Science, Mormonism, Judaism, and the Oriental religions. Doctrinal, textual, philosophic, psychological, and social aspects were interminably shuffled and rebalanced in successive DDC editions. According to one voice of reason:

> There surely have been inadequacies and religious biases in Dewey's Decimal Classification. Some of these faults are attributable to the personal peculiarities of Dewey himself; some to the kinds of libraries for which early editions of the system were designed; and some to the later editors of the scheme. Most of these biases are forgivable because they were inevitable—or at least human.
>
> Probably any general library classification is more likely to be—or seem—biased in religion than in any other discipline. Several factors account for this warpage: the large number of materials to be classified; the parochial and controversial vein of many books in the field; the fact that, traditionally, people are likely to be narrow-minded in religion—not considering beliefs other than their own to be particularly important. Any hierarchical classification is, as we have been reminded so often, always unsatisfactory to most users, but its faults are likely to be magnified when it is examined by religionists. On the whole then, it seems fair to conclude that the Decimal Classification's sections devoted to religion have stood up reasonably well against charges of opponents (Broadus 1970, 574–78).

There is no point to ponder belief. A battery of techniques was supplied in *DDC 18* to allow preferred treatment, with shorter numbers, for any belief. The options are summarized in Bloomberg and Weber (1976, 59). They include two permanently unassigned numbers for local use: 289.2 and 298.

Terminology changes show up regularly throughout the class, sometimes signifying conceptual shifts, but at other times merely conforming to modern usage.

Main class 200 should be labeled Theology, as Dewey did in the first edition. Religion is the worship of a god or gods; theology, their study. Many things other than gods are worshipped.

We do not wish to leave Dewey to heaven for the sin of placing the standard subdivisions of Christianity at the main class standard subdivision positions, i.e., at 201–209. He erred when he did it; subsequent editors have perpetuated the error. (All save Mary South, that is, editor of the *Dewey Decimal Classification for School Libraries* [a publication directed toward the United Kingdom], who placed the standard subdivisions of Christianity in 230, along with general works on Christianity.)

Outline and Details of Class 200

200	Religion
210	Philosophy and theory of religion
220	Bible
230	Christianity Christian theology
240	Christian moral and devotional theology
250	Local Christian church and Christian religious orders
260	Christian social and ecclesiastical theology
270	Historical, geographic, persons treatment of Christianity Church history
280	Denominations and sects of Christian church
290	Comparative religion and religions other than Christianity

Division 200: This division is used for the standard subdivisions of religion in general (200.1–.9). Standard subdivisions of Christianity have been moved from this division into 230, 260, or 270 in the continuing effort to remove the Christian bias in the Schedules.

Division 210: This division is used for the philosophy and theory of religion and contains those works in which religious convictions or viewpoints are achieved through "reason, observation of nature, and speculation instead of revelation" (Bloomberg and Weber 1976, 69). A further analysis of the breadth of the division shows that it includes the concepts of natural and philosophical theology. The standard subdivision, theory of philosophy of religion (210.1), is found in this section then 211–219 are concerned with concepts and characteristics of God, including such disparate "isms" as polytheism, monotheism, humanism, and skepticism in addition to creation, science and religion, theodicy, and humankind.

Division 220:   The Bible, the holy scriptures used by Judaism and Christianity, is found in this division. Standard subdivisions (220.01–.09) and generalities, such as sources and verification (220.1), are found in this very crowded section, followed by versions and translations (220.4–.5); introductions to the scriptures, literary and historical criticism (220.6); commentaries (220.7); nonreligious subjects in the scriptures (220.8); and ending the section with geography, history, chronology, persons of biblical lands and time (220.9). The Old Testament, or Tanakh, is covered next with general works (221) followed by the historical books (222), poetic books and wisdom literature (223), and prophetic books (224). The Manual suggests an optional arrangement for the Tanakh, or Jewish scriptures, which includes the Torah (222), Ketuvim (223), and Nevi'im (224). [The Manual indicates these as Nevi'im (223) and Ketuvim (224).] Christianity's New Testament is next with general aspects first (225), followed by the Gospels and Acts (226), the Epistles (227), Revelation (228), and concluding the division with Apocryphal or noncanonical works (229).

Division 230:   General aspects of Christianity and Christian theology are found in this division. Standard subdivisions of Christianity are first (230.002–.007), followed by standard subdivisions of Christian theology (230.01–.09), and doctrines of specific denominations and sects (230.1–.9). Aspects of Christian theology include God (231) and Jesus Christ and his family (232). In addition, this divisions covers human beings and their place in Christianity, including the creation, original sin, good and evil (233); salvation and grace (234); saints, angels, and devils (235); humankind's purpose and destiny (236); creeds (238); ending with arguments in defense of precepts of Christianity and attacks upon its detractors (239).

Division 240:   Christian moral (241) and devotional theology are found in this division. Included are meditations and prayers for devotional use (242); evangelical works (243); art in Christianity (246); church furnishing (247); spirituality, worship, and Christian life and practices (248–249).

Division 250:   This division is for the local Christian church and the religious orders. Standard subdivisions are first (250.1–.9), then following are all aspects of the local church including preaching and sermons (251–252); pastoral life, duties, and administration (253–254, 259); and Religious orders (255).

Division 260:   This division covers Christian social and political roles (261); church organization and government (262); religious observances and worship (263–265); missions (266); organizations that are part of Christianity but not necessarily Christian organizations (267); religious education (268); and evangelism and pentecostalism end the division (269).

Division 270:   This division is used for the church history (271–273) and geographical treatment of Christianity (274–279).

Division 280:   Denominations and sects of the Christian church are in this division, with the standard subdivisions (280.01–.09) and branches (280.2–.4) first, followed by early and Eastern churches (281); Roman Catholic Church (282); Anglican churches (283); and Protestant denominations and other sects (284–289).

Division 290:   The last division of this class contains comparative religion (291) and all other religious faiths with classical religions first (292); germanic religions (293); Buddhism, Jainism, Hinduism, and Sikhism (294); Zoroastrianism (295). The other two great religions that, besides Christianity, recognize the Old Testament's Abraham are Judaism (296) and Islam, which shares a section with Babism and Bahai Faith (297). All other religions are crowded into 299, arranged by ethnic orientation (299).

The Number Building Process

Example 1.   A work on Calvinistic Baptist missionaries.

The Relative Index lists Missionaries at 291.720 92 and Christian missionaries at 266.0092. Because this piece is about a specific Christian denomination, the base number must be

266

The next step is to look in the Schedules under 266.

266	**Missions**
.009	Historical, geographic, persons treatment

Do not use for foreign missions originating in specific continents, countries, localities; class in 266.023. Do not use for historical, geographic, persons treatment of missions of specific denominations and sects; class in 266.1–266.9.

The work is not about a foreign mission from a specific location; however, it is about missions from a specific denomination.

.1–.9	**Missions of specific denominations and sects**

Add to base number 266 the numbers following 28 in 281–289, e.g., Anglican missions 266.3; Anglican missions serving Africa 266.36.

Sections 281–289 are for specific denominations and sects of the Christian church. Baptist churches are found at 286.1–.5.

286	**Baptist, Disciples of Christ, Adventist churches**
.1	**Regular (Calvinistic) Baptists**
.2	**Freewill Baptists**

.3   **Seventh-Day Baptists**
.4   **Old School Baptists**
.5   **Other Baptist churches and denominations**

The notation for Calvinistic Baptists is 286.1. Following the instructions, we drop 28 and add the rest (61) to 266.

266.61

Because this work is about individuals in the mission rather than the mission itself, Table 1 (Standard Subdivisions) notations are now applied. The work is about more than one missionary, so it is a Collected persons treatment.

—0922   Collected persons treatment

266.610922 *The Dream Builders*

Example 2. A work on religion and an abused wife.

This is a more difficult concept to class. The Relative Index has no reference for abused wives but does for abused children:

Abused children	305.906 945
pediatrics	618.928 582 23
social group	305.906 945
Social theology	291.178 327 1
Christianity	261.832 71
social welfare	362.76

Reviewing the work once more, we find the specific topic to be Christianity's suggestions or help to abused wives. Obviously, 261 looks closer, and we find there the following:

261		**Social theology and interreligious relations and attitudes**
.8		**Christianity and socioeconomic problems**
	.832	Social welfare problems and services
	.8327	Abuse within the family
	.83271	Child abuse and neglect
	.83272	Sexual abuse
	.83273	Adults who were victims of abuse as children
	.833	Crime
	.834	Relations of age groups, the sexes, social classes, language groups, ethnic groups
	.835	Sexual relations, marriage, divorce, family
	.836	Ecology and population

Even though the abuse of wives is considered a social problem, these choices are more in the nature of the Christian attitude toward wife abuse, which is really not the subject matter of the book, so none of these would be appropriate. Retreating to the outline of 200, a possibility is found in 240, Christian moral and devotional theology.

241	Moral theology
242	Devotional literature
243	Evangelistic writings for individuals and families
246	Use of art in Christianity
247	Church furnishings and related articles
248	Christian experience, practice, life
249	Christian observances in family life

Studying the division breakdowns, Christian experience, practice, life (248) may be appropriate.

248

Looking the division up in the Schedules, we find the following:

248	Christian experience, practice, life
.2	Religious experience
.3	Worship
.4	Christian life and practice
.5	Witness bearing
.6	Stewardship
.8	Guide to Christian life for specific classes of persons
.82	Children
.83	Adolescents and college students
.84	Adults
.843	Women
.843 2–.843 9	Women by marital status

Add to base number 248.843 the numbers following —865 in notation 08652–08659 from Table 1, e.g., guides for wives 248.8435.

.85	Persons in late adulthood
.86	Persons experiencing illness, trouble, bereavement
.88	Occupational classes
.89	Religious groups

The best choice, close but not exact, seems to be Women by marital status, at .8432–.8439. After the Add instructions, we find the following in Table 1:

—086 52	Single persons
—086 53	Separated and divorced persons
—086 54	Widowed persons
—086 55	Married persons
—086 59	Polygamous persons

The obvious choice is —08655, for Married persons. As directed, we use only the number following 865, which is 5, and add it to the base number 248.843 to get the following:

248.8435   *He Hits*

DDC 21 Revisions

Extensive work has been done in the 200 class to reduce the Western Christian bias in religion, which may continue in new editions because of the increasing use of the Schedules by a broader range of libraries. Many subdivisions have been discontinued in favor of uniting aspects under a broader heading.

Summary *(DDC 20)*		Summary *(DDC 21)*	
210	**Natural theology**	**210**	**Philosophy and theory of religion**
230	**Christian theology**	**230**	**Christianity Christian theology**
250	**Christian orders and local church**	**250**	**Local Christian church and Christian religious orders**
260	**Christian social theology**	**260**	**Christian social and ecclesiastical theology**
270	**Christian church history**	**270**	**Historical, geographic, persons treatment of Christianity; Church history**
280	**Christian denominations**	**280**	**Denominations and sects of and sects Christian church**
290	**Other and comparative religions**	**290**	**Comparative religion and religions other than Christianity**

Special topics (204) has been discontinued because of lack of meaning in this context. Standard subdivisions of religion have been revised to reduce the Christian bias and to recognize their more general applications. Many aspects under 200.1 (.11 Systems, .13 Values, .15 Scientific principles, and .19 Psychology of religion) now include what was formerly Natural theology (210). However, Classification (.12) and Language and communication (.14) are merged under Philosophy and theory of religion, now 210.

200	Public relations for religion (659.292) is now found here.
200.11	Systems was consolidated here from 210.11 and 291.011.
200.13	Value has been consolidated here from 210.13 and 291.013.
200.15	Scientific principles was united here from 210.15 and 291.015.
200.19	The Psychology of religion from 210.19 and 291.019 were merged here.
200.2–.3	Standard subdivisions for Miscellany and Dictionaries, encyclopedias, and concordances were merged here from 291.02–.03, Comparative religion.
200.5	Serial publications was consolidated here from 291.05.

200.7   Education, research, and related topics of Comparative religion (291.07) was consolidated here.

200.8   History and description with respect to kinds of persons from Comparative religion (291.08) was merged here.

200.9   Historical, geographic, persons treatment of Comparative religion (291.09) has been consolidated here.

Philosophy and theory of religion (210) encompasses those beliefs that find their justification in the natural world, rather than from revelation or the teaching of scriptures. Natural and philosophical theologies are found in this class. Facets from both 200, Religion, and 291, Comparative religion, have been consolidated here. Much of Science and religion, 215, has been reduced or relocated. Many of the subdivisions have been discontinued in favor of using the broader class of Science and religion (Mathematics, .1; Life on other worlds and space flight, .24–.25; Chemistry and geology, .4–.5; and Archaeology and technology, .8–.9).

210   Philosophy and theory of religion was moved from 200.1 and joined with that of Comparative religion (291.01) to encompass all non-Christian aspects.

210.14   The Language and communication of religion in general (200.14) and Comparative religion (291.014) are now combined here under Philosophy and theory of religion.

214   Concepts of good and evil (216) were shifted here under Theodicy, "vindication of God's justice and goodness in permitting existence of evil and suffering."

215.7   Paleontology (215.6) was moved here under Life sciences. The subdivisions for anthropology, ethnology, biology, and natural history (215.72–.74) are also encompassed by this number.

In keeping with a general Christian emphasis, one whole division (220) is dedicated to the Bible, with its apocryphal works, versions, and commentaries. Other religious works are all crowded into division 290. The separation of the Old Testament (Tanakh) (221), from sources of Judaism (296.1) has been unfortunate; however, there is a reference to see 221 "For Torah and sacred scripture (Tanakh, Old Testament)." *DDC 21* has only minor changes in the division for the Bible.

223   Ketuvim (Hagiographa, Writings) was relocated to the Poetic books of the Old Testament from the Old Testament in general (221.042).

229.6   Song of the Three Children (229.5) has been moved here with Prayer of Manasseh, and Susanna, Bel and the Dragon.

Comprehensive works on Christianity were moved from 200 and integrated with Christian theology here to produce a more cohesive and orderly arrangement of the subject, as well as to reduce the Christian emphasis in the Schedules. Christian mythology (204.5) was relocated here also. Standard subdivisions of Christianity were formerly sections, but in the drive to reduce the Christian emphasis, these have been shifted here: Miscellany, 202 to 230.002; Dictionaries, encyclopedias, concordances, 203 to 230.003; Serial publications, 205 to 230.005; and Education, research and related topics of Christianity, 207 to 230.007.

230.01	The Philosophy and theory of Christianity was repositioned from 201.
230.01–	Standard subdivisions of Specific types of Christian theology (230.0401–.0409) and Specific schools and systems of theology (230.04601–.04609) are now merged under the broader category of Christianity.
230.071	Education in Christianity (207.1) is now found here.
230.0711	Higher education in Christianity in specific continents, countries, and localities in the modern world (207.4–.9) have been shifted to 230.07114–.07119.
232.91	Sanctity, virtues, and spiritual powers (232.915–.916) have been moved here under Mary, mother of Jesus.
232.92	Circumcision, massacre of innocents, and the flight into Egypt (232.924–.926) are now found here under the Birth, infancy, and childhood of Jesus.
234.13	Gifts of and baptism in the Holy Spirit (234.12) has been shifted here under Spiritual gifts.
234.132	Speaking in tongues, or Glossolalia (248.29), has been consolidated here under Spiritual gifts.
236.4	Limbo of fathers and infants (236.6, .7) are merged here under the Intermediate state.
239.01–	Standard subdivisions of Apologetics and polemics have been shifted here from 239.001–.009.
239.7	Polemics against deists (239.5), encyclopedists (239.6), scientists and materialists (239.8), and secular humanists (239.9) are merged here under Polemics against rationalists, agnostics, apostates, and atheists in postapostolic times.

The divisions for Christian moral and devotional theology (240) and Local Christian church and Christian religious orders (250) have not been modified in *DDC* 21. There have been some revisions in the sections and subdivisions but nothing of great substance. Activities of the local church (259) has become the Pastoral care of families, specific kinds of persons and has been expanded.

241.3	Sins against the Holy Spirit (241.32) now is included here under Sin and vices.
241.5	Precepts of the church (241.57) is discontinued and included in this more general aspect, Codes of conduct.
242.36	Ascension Day (242.37) moved here logically under the Easter season.
242.6	Prayers and meditations for church year, other Christian feast and fast days for specific classes of persons (242.3), and Prayers and meditations for daily use for specific classes of persons (242.2) are merged here.
242.72	Prayers of praise (Doxologies, 242.721) and prayers of faith, thanksgiving, penitence, petition (242.723–.726) are now found here under Specific types of prayers.
252.63	Texts of sermons for Ascension Day (252.67) are now found here under the Easter season.
253.7	Pastoral methods now encompasses those specific types of activities formerly found in 259.8 and outdoor pastoral methods (253.73).
259	Pastoral care of families, of specific kinds of persons was Activities of the local church. This section has also been expanded.
259.088	Occupational and religious groups under History and description with respect to kinds of persons is a new number.
259.12	Family counseling is a new number.
259.13	Premarital counseling is a new number.
259.14	Marriage counseling is a new number.
259.25	Pastoral care of young adults is a new number.

Christian social theology (260) has been broadened to include Ecclesiastical theology, which has resulted in many changes. Facets have been moved here from other places, and there has been much shifting about within the division. In addition, The Young Men's and Women's Christian Associations have been thoroughly revised. Staff and departments (267.34–.35 and 267.54–.55), Program and objectives, and buildings and equipment (267.31–.32 and 267.51–.52) are consolidated under 267.3 and 267.5 respectively. Organizations and management (267.306 and 267.506) now include Organization and management, formerly at 267.33 and 267.53. Historical, geographic, persons treatment (267.309 and 267.509) are moved to 267.39 and 267.59.

260	Organizations of Christianity (206) are now found here.
263.041	Pilgrimages were moved here from 248.463.

263.3	Sunday observance (263.4) has been relocated here.
263.93	Ascension Day (263.97) is merged with Easter season here.
264	Creeds, confessions of faith, sermons, exhortations, instructions (264.5–.6) are now incorporated here in Public worship.
264.03	Rubrics (264.032) and Texts of ordinal, articles, creeds (264.037) are consolidated here under Public worship in the Anglican churches.
264.032	Texts of lectionary now includes the texts of epistles, Gospels (264.036).
264.23	Hymns now includes those hymns for devotional use of individuals and families (245).
267	Pious societies, sodalities, and confraternities moved here under Associations for religious work from 248.06.
267.3	Program and objectives, buildings and equipment (267.31–.32) and Staff and departments (267.34–.35) of YMCA were moved here.
267.306	Organizations and management of YMCA (267.33) were consolidated here.
267.39	Historical, geographic, persons treatment of YMCA (267.309) was shifted here.
267.5	Program and objectives, buildings and equipment (267.51–.52) and Staff and departments (267.54–.55) of YWCA were moved here.
267.506	Organizations and management of YWCA (267.53) were consolidated here.
267.59	Historical, geographic, persons treatment of YWCA (267.509) was shifted here.
267.61	Young People's Society of Christian Endeavor (267.613) is now found here under Interdenominational and nondenominational associations.
268.6	The Value and use of textbooks, textbook method (268.61–.62) as well as Laboratory methods (268.68) are consolidated here under Methods of instruction and study.
269	Pentecostalism (269.4) is now found here under Spiritual Renewal.

The Historical, geographic, persons treatment of Christianity (209) is now found in 270 along with Church history, which is similar to Edition 19, in which the History and geography of the church were also found here. Historical periods are found in 270.1–.8; Treatment by continent, country, locality, formerly found in 270.093–.099, has been moved to 274–279.

270 SUMMARY

271	**Religious congregations and orders in church history**
272	**Persecutions in general church history**
273	**Doctrinal controversies and heresies in general church history**
274–279	**Treatment by continent, country, locality**

Christianity with respect to kinds of persons has been moved from 208 and is now found in 270.08 with Church history with respect to kinds of persons. The Historical, geographic, persons treatment of specific denominations and sects are found in 280, Denominations and sects of Christian church. There have been two relocations in this division:

280.042   The Ecumenical movement (270.82) was shifted here under Relations between denominations.

287.99   Church of the Nazarene (289.9) is now listed here under Churches related to Methodism.

By far, most of the changes in Religion are those in the division for Comparative religion and religions other than Christianity (290). These occur in all sections, with the most found in 296, Judaism. Many of them involve the relocations of Management and Organizations.

Comparative religion changes follow:

291.14   Classification of religions is consolidated here from both 200.12 and 210.12.

291.351   Pilgrimages has been moved here under Public worship from 291.446, Individual observances.

291.44   Guides to religious life (291.448) has been consolidated under Religious life and practice.

291.6   Management (200.68) was shifted here under Leaders and organization.

291.61   Leaders and their work now incorporates persons endowed with supernatural power (291.62), divinely inspired persons (291.63), and interpreters of religion (291.64).

291.65   Organizations (200.6, 291.06) are integrated here.

Organizations and management for Religions other than Christianity, 292–299, have been relocated from —06 to —6 for management and —65 for organizations.

Classical (Greek and Roman) religion changes follow:

292.65   Organizations was moved from 292.006.

Religions of Indic origin changes follow:

294.36   Management under Buddhism was shifted here from 294.306.

294.365   Under Buddhism, Organizations were moved from 294.306.

294.56   Management under Hinduism was shifted here from 294.506.

294.565   Under Hinduism, Organizations were moved from 294.506.

Judaism (296) has been revised and expanded, which often results in a simplified notation. Organizations are found in .67 rather than .65, which is Synagogues and congregations. An optional number, 296.11, is provided for the Books of Tanakh, which can be arranged to reflect the Jewish order.

296.09   Histories of specific synagogues (296.8) are now found here.

296.09013 Earliest Judaism, to 586 B.C., now includes 999–586 B.C., which was 296.09014.

296.09014 The Second Temple period, 586 B.C.–70 A.D., now includes 1–70 A.D., which was 296.09015.

296.12   There have been a number of additions under Talmudic literature including .120092 persons and orders of Mishnah, which are now in 296.1231–.1237, new numbers.

296.124   Individual orders and tractates under Palestinian Talmud are at 296.1241–.1247, new numbers.

296.125   Individual orders and tractates under Babylonian Talmud are at 296.1251–.1257, new numbers.

296.162   Zohar is a new number.

296.18   Halakhah (Legal literature) now includes Early rabbinical legal writings and comprehensive works on rabbinical writings to 1400 (296.17). In addition, persons are now found at 296.18092, a new number.

296.181   Legal writing of Maimonides is a new number.

296.1812 Mishneh Torah is a new number.

296.311   Under God there are now a series of new numbers, from 296.3112–.3118.

296.336   Messianism is a new number.

296.35   Apologetics and polemics is a new number.

296.36   Ethics has been relocated here, a new number, from 296.385.

296.37   Judaism and secular disciplines were moved here, a new number, from 296.3875. There is also a series of new numbers from 296.371–.377 for aspects of this subject.

296.38	Social theology (296.387) has been relocated here under Judaism and social sciences.
296.382	Judaism and politics (296.3877) is now located here, a new number.
296.3827	International affairs, war and peace (296.38787), have been relocated here, a new number.
296.383	Judaism and economics was moved to this new number from 296.38785.
296.39	Judaism and other systems of belief was shifted to this new number from 296.3872.
296.396	Judaism and Christianity is a new number.
296.397	Judaism and Islam is a new number.
296.412	Prohibited activity on the Sabbath is a new number.
296.4315	Rosh Hashanah (New Year) is a new number.
296.4391	Festivals, holy days, fasts associated with the land of Israel is a new number.
296.4434	Bat mitzvah is a new number.
296.4443	Interreligious marriage is a new number.
296.4444	Divorce rites and traditions is a new number.
296.446	Synagogue dedication is a new number.

Liturgy and prayers for the Sabbath (296.41) have been relocated to 296.45 under Liturgy and prayers, as have comprehensive works on worship (296.72). Liturgy and prayers for occasions that generally occur once in a lifetime (296.43–.44) have been moved to 296.453–.454.

296.45	There are new numbers under Liturgy and prayers from 296.4504–.454.
296.46	Use of the arts and symbolism now include new numbers ranging from 296.461–.462.
296.47	Sermons and preaching (Homiletics) has been moved here, a new number, from 296.42.
296.48	Pilgrimages and sacred places (through 296.483–.489) now are new numbers.
296.49	Traditions, rites, public services of ancient Judaism to 70 A.D. includes new numbers through 296.495.
296.61	Persons treatment of writers on leaders and their work (296.61092) is now found here.

296.67   Organizations under Judaism (296.06) and Young Men's and Women's Hebrew Associations (296.673–.675) are now found here.

296.69   Outreach activity for the benefit of converts and nonobservant Jews is a new number.

296.7   Religious life and practice (296.74) is now found here under Religious experience, life, practice.

296.7086   Persons by miscellaneous social characteristics is a new number.

296.714   Conversion is a new number.

296.715   Return of Jews from non-observance to religious observance is a new number.

296.74   Social theology of marriage and family was moved here from 296.387835.

296.742   Observance of laws of family purity is a new number.

296.75   Ritual bath (Mikveh) is a new number.

296.8   Denominations and movements have new numbers for Sadducees (.813), Essenes (.814), Samaritans (.817).

296.8341   Reform Judaism was shifted here, a new number, from 296.8346.

A lot of attention has been given to revising and expanding 297, Islam, Babism, Bahai faith. The logic of the Dewey system is so evident that William Collins created an arrangement for the Baha'i World Centre Library's collection in Haifa, Israel, in which he used "standard Dewey devices," such as the Tables, because many other Baha'i libraries already used the Dewey system (Collins 1993, 104).

Organizations were moved to .65, and Management moved to .6 from 297.06. Mythology (297.19) was discontinued because it has no meaning in its context, Sources of Islam.

297.1   Sources of Islam was also social theology, relations, attitudes of Islam. Also, oral traditions (297.13) are now found here under Sources of Islam.

297.12   There are now a series of new numbers under Koran and Hadith, from .12203 to .1228999.

297.1226   Interpretation and criticism (Exegesis) now includes Symbolism, typology, harmonies, and literary criticism (297.12264–.12266) and Mythological, astronomical interpretations (297.12268).

297.14	Fiqh in relation to religious and ceremonial laws and decisions (340.59) is now consolidated here under Religious and ceremonial laws and decisions.
297.18	Stories, legends, parables, proverbs, anecdotes told for religious edification is a new number.
297.21	God and spiritual beings includes a series of new numbers through .2118.
297.22	Humankind includes new numbers through .227.
297.24	Other doctrines have new numbers through .2465.
297.26	Islam and secular disciplines was relocated here, a new number, from 297.197. In addition, there are new numbers under this subject through .267.
297.27	Islam and social services is a new number. In addition, there are more new numbers under the topic through .273.
297.28	Islam and other systems of belief was moved here, a new number, from 297.197. There are also new numbers for aspects of this topic through .289.
297.29	Polemics against pagans and heathens (297.291), against other religions (297.295), and against rationalists, agnostics, and atheists (297.297) are now included here under Apologetics and polemics.
297.3	Islamic worship was Islamic public worship and other practices. Comprehensive works on Islamic worship, non-Sufi worship, Islamic private worship, non-Sufi private worship (297.43) were repositioned here.
297.31	Pillars of Islam was moved to this new number from 297.5.
297.34	Shahāda was shifted to this new number from 297.51.
297.35	Non-Sufi pilgrimages and comprehensive works on Islamic pilgrimages (297.446) and rites and ceremonies associated with sacred places and pilgrimages (297.38) were merged here under Sacred places and pilgrimages.
297.351	Mosques is a new number.
297.352	Hajj (pilgrimage to Mecca) was moved to this new number under Islamic worship from 297.55.
297.353	Sacred places and pilgrimages treatment by specific continents, countries, localities (297.35093–.35099) are now found in new numbers here through 297.359.
297.36	Rites and ceremonies associated with special days and seasons (297.38) are consolidated here.

297.362	Ṣawm Ramaḍān (annual fast of Ramadan) (297.53) is now consolidated here, a new number.
297.37	Sermons and preaching is a new number.
297.382	Prayer and meditation is a new number.
297.3822	Ṣalāt (Prayer five times daily) (297.52) is a new number.
297.3824	Texts of prayers and meditations is a new number.
297.39	Divination and occultism (297.32–.33) are now found under this new number.
297.4	Sufism has a series of new numbers for topics under it from .41 through .482. Specific aspects of Sufism (297.1–.3, .5–.7) as well as Sufi religious experience (297.42) are now located here.
297.435	Sufi pilgrimages was moved here from 297.446.
297.44	Guides to Sufi religious life (297.448) has been moved here.
297.446	Now includes Sufi ascetic practices (297.447).
297.45	Sufi fasting was moved here from 297.447.
297.5	Islamic moral theology and religious experience, life, practice has a series of new numbers, from .56 through .577.
297.57	Non-Sufi and comprehensive works on Islamic religious experience, life, practice (297.4) and Non-Sufi and comprehensive guides to religious life (297.448) were consolidated here.
297.577	Islamic social theology of marriage and family (297.1978358) has been moved here under Religious experience, life, practice.
297.61	Caliphate and Imamate (297.24 and 297.65) and Persons who study and write about the role, function, duties of religious leaders (297.61092) are now located here under Leaders and their work.
297.63	Muḥammad the Prophet has new numbers from .63092 through .635.
297.64	Muḥammad's family and companions has been expanded, with new numbers from .642 through .648.
297.65	Organizations of Islam were moved here from 297.06.
297.7	Protection and propagation of Islam has been expanded, with new numbers from .74 through .77083.
297.833	Ibadites is a new number.
297.834	Motazilites is a new number.

Other changes in the class of Religion follow:

Religions originating among Black Africans and people of Black African
   descent:
299.64   Practices (299.65) were consolidated here.
Religions of other origin:
299.936   Dianetics (158.9) was relocated here with Scientology.

Exercises in the Use of Class 200

Answers to these exercises can be found in the appendix.
1.   A work on the effect that evangelism has had on the South.
2.   Ancient Daoist scriptures translated into English.
3.   A work on a Japanese religious ritual for aborted fetuses.
4.   A work on Hindu goddesses–related sexuality and violence.
5.   A work on the religious theories of creation.
6.   A work on the Taoist religion.

Literature Cited

Bloomberg, Marty, and Hans Weber. 1976. *An introduction to classification and
   number building in Dewey.* Ed. John Phillip Immroth. Littleton, CO: Libraries Unlimited.

Broadus, Robert N. 1970. Dewey and religion. *Library Resources & Technical
   Services* 14 (4): 574–78.

Collins, W. P. 1993. Classification for materials on the Baha'i Religion: A "B200"
   schedule based on the Dewey Decimal Classification. *Cataloging & Classification Quarterly* 16 (4): 103–21; 18 (2): 71–86.

Dewey, Melvil. 1996. *Dewey Decimal Classification and Relative Index.* 21st ed.
   Vol. 2. Albany, NY: Forest Press.

Class 300
Social Sciences

Introduction

Social sciences is a wide-ranging class that includes such diverse subjects as general statistics, law, military science, and etiquette. One may say that it is a catchall for categories not covered by the other nine classes. It ranks second in size to Technology (Applied sciences), but in complexity it ranks first.

Placing Economics (330) between Political science (320) and Law (340) and distant from Commerce, communications, transportation (380) is regrettable, but it would not serve a useful purpose to revamp the divisions (and put the users in a tizzy) to rectify the predicament. Situating public administration and military science in the same division is also puzzling and almost amusing. Is it a comment on our civilization that implies that if the government does not function properly, the military will step in and assume the authority, as well as the reverse, where military juntas are overthrown and constitutional governments instated? A parallel paradox is figuring out if social problems and services are the same as associations (360). And what relationship is there between penal institutions and insurance, or social problems and clubs?

Customs, etiquette, folklore (390) is the oddest of the DDC divisions. Customs is a part of culture and consequently belongs in 306, Culture and institutions. Costume and personal appearance both belong in the 640s, Home economics and family living. Folklore is also culture, but Folk literature belongs in literature, not the Social sciences, for it is a compendium of literary works of the imagination. Etiquette (little ethics) belongs with "big ethics," 170. And the Customs of war and diplomacy are here rather than with war in 355 and diplomacy in 327.

All and all, it is a strange and badly conceived class. Valiant efforts have been made to fix the problems, but these have always failed, perhaps because of the impact upon the users. Even when the redoubtable Benjamin A. Custer tried to remove folk literature to the 800s, he was unable to win the battle. The only explanation for these paradoxes is that this is the resting ground for the misfits that do not belong in other classes and have some sort of relationship to society, thus creating this strange mélange of topics that are merged together like adopted children in a comfortable home of disparate members.

Outline and Details of Class 300

300	Social sciences
310	General statistics
320	Political science (Politics and government)
330	Economics
340	Law
350	Public administration and military science
360	Social problems and services; associations
370	Education
380	Commerce, communications, transportation
390	Customs, etiquette, folklore

Division 300:   As usual, the standard subdivisions of social sciences are found in the first division (300.1–.9) followed by books in sociology and anthropology that are general in nature (301). More specific topics come next, such as interpersonal and social relationships, and nontechnical concepts of communication (302); socialization by various parts of society and studies on all aspects of social change (303); natural and demographic factors impacting society, domestic emigration and migration (304); specific groups that make up societies (305); the beliefs, values, mores, and institutions that make up societies (306); and the study of communities (307).

Division 310:   This division contains books on the various statistics of societies, such as censuses. Statistics of specific subjects are found with the subject plus the notation from Table 1 for statistics (—021), but statistical data not related to a specific topic are found here (310) followed by general statistics of specific locations in the modern world (314–319).

Division 320:   This division is used for political science, or the study of politics and government. The first section contains standard subdivisions (320.01–.09), and general aspects of the discipline, such as the structure and functions of government, and political conditions (320.1–.9). The various types of government are found in the next section (321) followed by relationship of the government to its governed peoples (322) and their rights (323). Books on political parties and elections are next (324) followed by the international movement of peoples, including colonization (325); political aspects of slavery and emancipation (326); relationships between countries (327); concluding the division are books about laws, lawmaking, and the governmental bodies that are responsible for them (328).

Division 330:   This division is used for economics, the first section being reserved for standard subdivisions (330.01–.09). The "systems" part of the first standard subdivision (—011) is in a separate section (330.1) as are the geographic and historic treatments of economic conditions (330.9). The next section is reserved for topics concerning the work force (331), followed by books on banking and money (332). The next section is used for economic aspects of natural resources, including land and forms of energy (333), then various types of economic cooperation in banking, housing, and other forms (334) and all types of socialism (335). Finance of governments is in the next section (336), followed by international economic cooperation of governments, policies, and relations (337). All types of economic production are in the next to last section (338), and the division ends with economics on a more universal scale, such as the distribution of wealth and aspects of the national product, macroeconomics (339).

Division 340:   The next division is used for law or jurisprudence, and like the previous division, the standard subdivisions (340.02–.09) are in the first section. However, philosophy and theory of law is separate (340.1) and found with general aspects (340.2–.9). The next section is reserved for international law (341) and the remaining sections encompass specific kinds of law: laws that are constitutionally based and those dealing with government duties and responsibilities (342); military law, public property, tax law, law of commerce (343); law concerning the work force, education, and other social and cultural activities (344); all aspects of criminal law (345); noncriminal law involving persons (346); civil trials and procedures (347); statutes and regulations (348); and the division ends with laws and regulations of specific areas (349).

Division 350:   This division holds such unlikely companions as the executive branch of government, civil service, and military and naval sciences. Standard subdivisions of public administration are found in 351 (351.01–.09), followed by administration of areas in general (351.1) and specific areas (351.3–.9). Finances, personnel, and other aspects of public administration (352–354) are in the next section (352), followed by administration of specific services or functions (353) and of the economy and environment (354). Military science in general is in the next section (355), followed by land-based services and warfare including the infantry (356.1); cavalries and mounted forces (357); missile and armed forces (358.1); engineering services (358.2); air and space warfare and forces (358.4 and .8) complete the section. The last section is used for sea forces and warfare (359), including marine forces (359.96).

Division 360: This division is reserved for societies' problems and services available (361–365) and associations (366–369). In the first section, standard subdivisions for social problems and services (361.001–.008) are followed by free and fee-based services, then material and guidance assistance (361.02–.06). General aspects of these services, such as social, private, governmental, and community actions (361.1–.9) conclude the section. Illnesses, disabilities, the poor, the aged, and other groups are in the next section (362), followed by public safety, housing, environmental, and population problems (363); and crime, its prevention, and the treatment of criminals are in the next two sections (364–365); associations begin with philanthropic and social organizations (366–367), followed by insurance, which is a type of mutual help association (368); and the division ends with patriotic, military, racial, ethnic, and clubs for youths (369).

Division 370: Education is found in the next division, standard subdivisions being in the first section (370.1–.9), followed by schools, including teachers, students, the physical plant, and special education (371). Four out of the next five sections contain works about the levels of education, beginning with elemental education (372), then secondary education (373), and adult education (374). General aspects of curricula are found next (375), followed by higher education (378), and the division concludes with financial and policy issues (379).

Division 380: The next to last division is used for trade, communications, and transportation. The first section is reserved for standard subdivisions (380.01–.09) and books on trade in general (380.1), followed by domestic trade (381), and trade between countries (382) to conclude that subject. The next section begins communication with intercourse by mail (383), then communication by wire (384.1, .3, .6), wireless methods (384.5), and motion pictures (384.8). Railroads (385) begin transportation, followed by inland water transportation (386); marine, air, and space transportation (387); roads, local transportation, and pipelines (388); and concluding the division with systems of measurement and standardization (389).

Division 390: The final division is reserved for practices, manners, and conventions that are common to societies, in addition to tradition, lore, and folk tales common to a culture. The first section contains the standard subdivisions for the division (390.001–.009) and for customs (390.01–.09), followed by practices and conventions of social classes and those of occupations (390.1–.4). Works that are concerned with people's clothing and other ways that they adorn themselves are in the second section (391), followed by practices and conventions concerning the stages of life from birth to marriage and home (392), and to death (393). Conventions involving such diverse activities as consumption of food, drink, and drugs, holidays and other special days, recreation, suicide, and cannibalism are all in the next section (394). Manners comes next (395), followed by folk literature, riddles, proverbs, and rhyming games (398). Customs of war and diplomacy conclude the class.

The Number Building Process

Example 1.   A work on divorce in Virginia.

The Relative Index shows that divorce is classed in 306.89. However, this book is more about divorce law, so looking further in the index we find divorce law at 346.0166. Reviewing the schedules we find:

>346.0166   *Divorce, annulment, separation
>   Subdivisions are added for divorce, annulment, separation
>   together; for divorce alone

>*Add as instructed under 342–347

Looking under the add instructions we find the following:

>093–099   Treatment by limited area within a jurisdiction
>   Law limited to specific jurisdiction or area is classed
>   under the jurisdiction before indicating the subject of
>   a branch of law, e.g., criminal courts of Australia
>   345.9401, *not* 345.01094. Further instructions are given
>   under 342–349

Now moving to the instruction under 342–349 we find the following:

>To show a specific branch, a specific subject, or a kind of original
>material, arrange the elements as follows, using criminal courts of
>Australia as an example:
>   Base number: 34
>   Branch of law: Criminal law, 5
>   Jurisdiction or area: Australia, 94
>   Facet indicator: 0*
>   Subordinate subject in branch of law: Courts, 1
>   The complete number is 345.9401

>*Add 00 for standard subdivisions; see instructions at beginning of Table 1

Following these directions we build the number.

>   Base number: 34
>   Branch of law: Private law, 6
>   Jurisdiction or area: Virginia

Looking up Virginia in Table 2 we find that it is —755.

346.755

> Facet indicator: 0*

Because we are not adding Standard subdivisions we ignore the instruction at *.

346.7550

> Subordinate subject in branch of law: Divorce, .[0]166

346.7550166   *Divorce in Virginia*

Example 2.   A work about the U.S. Marines.

The Relative Index indicates that the Marines (Armed forces) is found at 359.96.

359.96
Reviewing the Schedules, we find the following:

> Add to base number 359.96 the numbers following 355 in 355.1–355.8 ...

Examining the piece, we find that it is only about the *U.S.* Marines. When we review 355 in the Schedules, we find the following Summary:

.1	**Military life and customs**
.2	**Military resources**
.3	**Organization and personnel of military forces**
.4	**Military operations**
.5	**Military training**
.6	**Military administration**
.7	**Military installations**
.8	**Military equipment and supplies (Matériel) Weapons (Ordnance)**

Because this is a general work about the U.S. Marines Corps, none of the notations are appropriate, so the next step would be to turn to the Tables, which can be added to any base number except where forbidden. We find in Table 1 that Treatment by specific continents, countries, localities; extraterrestrial worlds has the notations —093 through —099. And, as we found above, the notation for United States is 73.

359.960973   *Warriors: The U.S. Marines*

DDC 21 Revisions

In March 1976 the Decimal Classification Editorial Policy Committee (DDC) reviewed a survey report pinpointing 11 areas in need of extensive revisions, more than half (six) of which were in class 300 (Comaromi 1977, 21:94). Edition 20 began this mission with vast changes, but many were left for succeeding editions. Significant efforts have been made in Edition 21 to completely revise Public administration, 351–354, and Education, 370. Insurance (368) also contains notable modifications, and there was much shifting around in 324, The political process. The changes in Public administration and Education have been so extensive that detailed Comparative and Equivalence Tables are found in the back of Volume 1 of Edition 21. The comparison of the Summaries of Editions 20 and 21 belies the extent of the revisions in the class.

Summary *(DDC 20)*		Summary *(DDC 21)*	
320	Political science	320	Political science (Politics and government)
350	Public administration	350	Public administration and military science
360	Social services; associations	360	Social problems and services; associations
380	Commerce, communications, transport	380	Commerce, communications, transportation

Social sciences (300) has seen similar changes appear in Editions 19 and 20. Similar to Edition 20, these have been focused in the 305–306 area, which continued to present difficulties to DDC users. Many topics have been moved from 370, Education, in the revamping of that division. As seen in the Summaries, anthropology has been returned to its pre–Edition 20 state with general aspects (or comprehensive works) in 301 with Sociology, and specific topics have been mixed and blended throughout 302–307.

Summary *(DDC 20)*		Summary *(DDC 21)*	
301	Sociology	301	Sociology and anthropology
304	Relation of natural factors	304	Factors affecting social behavior
305	Social stratification	305	Social groups

Social interaction, or behavior, within and between groups is found in 302. Social workings that are necessary for the continuation of society are found in 303. The advancement of societies as affected by the environment is found in 304. People in classes or those that form a society, its culture, and institutions are found in 305. The basis, or essence, of society, its institutions, and culture are found in 306. Populations that exist in a specific geographically confined area and are considered as a whole are found in 307. Mass media's effect on specific subjects, other than social groups (302.23), is now found with the subject.

Other changes follow:

303.4   Disruptive changes, whether gradual (evolutionary) or abrupt (revolutionary) (303.42–.43), are now found here.

304.6   Population has been merged with Population size and composition (307.2).

305.242   Comprehensive works on young adults (305.235) are now found here.

305.8   Racial, ethnic, national groups associated with a specific language (305.7) are now found here.

306   Popular culture (306.1 and .4) has been shifted here. Comprehensive works on cultural institutions under 306.4 has been discontinued; 306 is now used instead.

306.43   Education as a specific aspect of culture has moved here from 370.19.

306.432   School and society now includes interdisciplinary works on Relations of teachers and society (371.104) and Relations of colleges and universities with society (378.103).

306.848   Gay marriage was moved here under Marriage and family from 306.738.

Division 310, Collections of general statistics, has no modifications in Edition 21. The big change here took place in Edition 20 when the heading became *General* statistics, such as a census, which clearly indicates the scope as it now exists. Statistics of populations, or demography, is now found scattered with the subjects, with the addition of —021. Demography in general is found in 304.6.

Political science (320) was a division cited as being in need of revision in the 1974 survey of the DDC in the United States and Canada. The political process or decisions regarding who is to wield power underwent a complete revision for Edition 19, additional changes in Edition 20, and rather substantial changes in Edition 21. Other changes follow:

321.00902 Medieval systems of government was moved here from 321.14.

321.0093   Ancient systems of government was moved here from 321.14.

321.1   Systems of government among nonliterate people (321.12) is now found here under Family based government.

321.8   Pure democracy (321.4) is now found here under Democratic government.

323.42   Comprehensive works on procedural rights (323.422) have been moved here under Equal protection of law.

323.60715 Citizenship programs in adult education (374.012) have been moved here under Citizenship.

324   The early termination of the chief executive before the expiration of his term (351.0036) and Method of selection of the chief executive (321 and 351.0034) were merged here under The political process.

324.24–.29 The notations 01 (General topics) and 08 (Other recent parties) have been added to the tables for Parties in specific countries in the modern world. Auxiliary party organizations (324.3094–.3099) is now 014. Other changes in the table are: Nominating party candidates (324.5094–.5099) is now 015; Nominating by caucuses (324.52094–.52099) is now 0152; Nominating by primaries (324.54094–.54099) is now 0154; and Nominating by conventions (324.56094–.56099) is now 0156.

324.63 Selecting presidents and governors in the United States (321.80420973) and in the specific states (321.80420974–.80420979, .804209969) are consolidated here under 324.630973–.630979, Electoral systems.

325.3 Colonial policy (325.31) is now found under Colonization.

327.11 Specific topics of International relations for specific nations (327.3–.9) were moved here through —.17.

327.174 Disarmament (355.03) and arms control are consolidated here, as well as Problems of arms limitation and of verifying arms-control treaty provisions for specific kinds of weapons (355.82).

327.1743 Problems of arms limitations and of verifying arms-control treaty provisions for specific kinds of naval weapons (359.82) are now found here under conventional weapons limitation, a new number.

327.1745 Chemical and biological disarmament is a new number.

327.1747 Nuclear disarmament is a new number.

328 Legislative bodies (328.3) have been moved here under The legislative process.

328.0601 Interparliamentary unions (328.30601) has been relocated under International organizations.

328.3 Specific topics of legislative reform (328.304) are now found here.

328.304 Legislative reform (328.4042) has been moved here.

328.3347 Proportional representation (324.63) was consolidated here.

328.36 Auxiliary organizations (of legislative bodies) have been moved here under Internal organization and discipline, from 328.361.

328.37 Enacting public laws (328.378) are now included here under Enactment of legislation.

328.378 Enactment of special types of legislation now includes Procedures for legislative enactment of budgets (351.7223).

In the previous edition of this book, John Phillip Comaromi listed Economics (330) as needing revisions second only to sections 301–307. Many changes, some sweeping in scope, were made in both Editions 20 and 21, especially section 333, which was changed from Land economics to Economics of land and energy; and 333.95 Biological resources, which was revised and expanded.

330   Interdisciplinary works on economic rights (323.46) is now found here under Economics.

331.011   Employment rights (323.46) is now merged here under Rights and position of labor.

331.1109   The Geographic distribution of the Labor force and market (331.111) has been merged here with the Historic and persons treatment.

332.042   International capital transactions (382.173) and International currency movements (382.174) are consolidated here under International finance.

332.67208   Domestic investment by specific kinds of individuals (332.67255) is now found here.

333.95   Biological resources has expanded to list the different species in new numbers, from .9522 through .9592–.9598.

333.954   Comprehensive works on mammals (333.959) were moved here under Animals.

333.956   Marine biological resources (333.952) is now found here under Fishes.

334.0601   International associations of cooperatives (334.0919) has been moved here.

338.06   Industrial productivity (338.09) is now found here under Production efficiency.

338.52   Price determination in international markets (382.1044) was moved here under Prices.

338.91   International development and growth (337) is now found only here.

339.01   Philosophy and theory (339.3) is now found here under Macroeconomics and related topics.

There have long been questions about the structure of Law (340), and indecision has wreaked havoc on the division.

When work on the 340s began, it was thought that there were three ways to arrange the materials in it. Using traditional Dewey practice, jurisdiction could be attached to type of law by means of —09. Thus, 345.0973 would be used for a work on criminal law in the United States. A second method was to add jurisdiction directly to 34, thus gathering law books together first by jurisdiction and then by type of law, as law is generally studied [i.e., 347.305 would be the number of criminal law in the United States]. A third way was to add jurisdiction directly to type of law [i.e., 345.73 for the same subject as above]. This would be followed by standard subdivisions or the special subdivisions peculiar to that type of law. Of the three ways, the third was the second choice of librarians in the United States, who preferred arrangement by the —09 method, and of librarians in Great Britain and elsewhere outside the United States, who preferred arrangement by jurisdiction first. British law librarians in particular called for a citation order that reflected the way law was actually studied—first by jurisdiction, then by type of law. The opinion of American law librarians—who usually do not use the DDC—and of American librarians of general collections—in which law is of secondary importance—weighed equally, however, in the scales of judgment. Hoping to alienate no one, the Decimal Classification Division opted for everyone's second choice, namely, number three. The editors reasoned that in this way no one would be offended by having someone else's first choice allowed. It appears, however, that two second choices do not make a first, for many British librarians have called for reversal of the decision in favor of the second method. The Americans have said little on the matter (Comaromi 1976, 594).

The British eventually broke with the Dewey preferred practice; they chose the option putting jurisdiction before type of law. Edition 20, under Comaromi's guidance, put in place the Division policy of assigning in the classification legal materials, both the British first choice (which the British National Bibliography uses) and the American second choice. The American first choice was never honored.

Several significant changes within the division 340 were not just local in effect. Procedural rights have been moved from 323.422 (Specific civil rights; limitation and suspension of civil rights) to the specific subject in law in this section. The law of specific Socioeconomic regions (340.0917) has been changed to the various regions (then the subject) from the subject (then the region). And Malpractice in a specific profession (346.033) is now found with the profession in 342–347. Finally, the Instructions for number building were moved from 340 (Law) to 342–347 or Branches of law; laws (statutes), regulations, cases; law of specific jurisdictions, areas, socioeconomic regions.

Other changes follow:

340.524   Law of traditional societies in the modern world (340.52094–.52099) is now consolidated here through 340.529.

340.59   Sharia (297.14) is now found here with fiqh under Islamic law.

341.66026 The Text of treaties limited to termination of war (341.026) was moved here under Treaties and cases.

341.751   Counterfeiting, forgery, alteration (International financial law) was moved here from 341.7519.

342.0412	Annexation of territory (342.0413) is now found here under Conduct of relations with foreign governments.
342.0664	Provisional courts (342.062) are now found here under Administrative courts and regulatory agencies.
342.068	Impeachment (351.993) has been moved here under Officials and employees.
342.07	Election procedures (342.075) are now found here under Election law.
342.1	Socioeconomic regions (342.00917) and specific subjects in them (342.02–.09) are now consolidated here.
343.05242	Wages and salaries now includes Social security taxes (344.02).
343.077	Comprehensive works on mining (343.0775) have been moved here under Mineral industries.
343.1	Socioeconomic regions (343.00917) and specific subjects in them (343.01–.09) have been combined here.
344.0411	Medical malpractice (346.0332) is now found here.
344.04633	Pollution of specific environments by specific pollutants (344.04634) is now merged here under Pollutants.
344.046336	Acid rain (344.04634) has been moved here.
344.047	Comprehensive works on public safety (344.05) were consolidated here under Safety.
344.078	Academic freedom (342.0853) is now located here under Teachers and teaching.
344.0791	Programs for exceptional students (344.0769) is now located here under Education of students belonging to specific groups.
344.099	Comprehensive works on gambling (344.0542) are now found here under Amusements.
344.1	Socioeconomic regions (344.00917) and specific subjects in them (344.01–.09) are now combined here.
345.1	Socioeconomic regions (345.00917) and specific subjects in them (345.01–.08) are now consolidated here.
346.0166	Marital property (346.04) is now found here under Divorce, annulment, separation.
346.042	Joint tenancy (346.0432) has been merged here under Kinds of interest in property.
346.1	Socioeconomic regions (346.00917) and Specific subjects in them (346.01–.09) are now consolidated here.

347.1   Socioeconomic regions (347.00917) and Specific subjects in them (347.01–.09) are now consolidated here.

348.1   Socioeconomic regions (348.00917) and Specific subjects in them (348.02–.05) are now consolidated here.

349.1   Law of socioeconomic regions (340.0917) is now found here.

There were few changes in Public administration (351–354) in Edition 20; however, there is no similarity to the division in Editions 20 and 21. The schedule is completely new with numbers reused for different purposes.

Summary *(DDC 20)*		Summary *(DDC 21)*	
350	Public administration	350	Public administration and military science
351	Of central governments	351	Public administration
352	Of local governments	352	General considerations of public administration
353	Of U.S. federal and state governments	353	Specific fields of public administration
354	Of specific central governments	354	Public administration of economy and environment

The focus has moved from the emphasis first on *which* government to the topics under Public administration, or from *place* to *what*. This change in focus has resulted in the reduction of the "United States bias" in which this country's governments were in a completely separate section (353). It is now a subdivision of one of the sections, just like New Zealand.

As indicated above, the revisions are so extensive that Tables were developed to guide the librarians using the Schedules; so it is not useful to repeat them here. A few items were moved completely out of Public administration, and these are listed at the beginning of 350. That leaves just those topics that were moved into Public administration to be listed below.

Other changes follow:

352.112   Management of the League of Nations was moved here from 341.22068 and 341.223.

352.113   The Secretariat (341.2324) and Management (341.233) of the United Nations are now consolidated here.

352.6211   International personnel administration (341.22–.24) is now consolidated here.

352.748   Public relations (659.2935) is now found here under Publicity activities.

353.15   Colonial administration (325.31) was moved here under Administration of non-self-governing territories.

353.824   Financial administration of agencies supporting public education (379.11) is now found here under Financial administration of public education.

353.88284 Government commissions on standards and accreditation in higher education (379.158) was moved here under Higher education.

There have been significant revisions to Military science also.

Summary *(DDC 20)*		Summary *(DDC 21)*
358	**Other specialized forces and services**	**358** **Air and other specialized forces and warfare; engineering and related services**

Like its civilian counterpart, Military administration (355.6) has been revised and expanded. The table for sections 356–359 also has been changed with administration (6) now including Administration of specific kinds of equipment and supplies and Supply and equipment management (previously 8 and 8068).

Standard subdivisions of weapons were moved to 355.801–.805 from 355.8201–.8205 under Military science, and to 359.801–.805 from 359.8201–.8205 in Naval forces.

Other changes follow:

355.07   Research in Military science (355.0072) and comprehensive works on military aspects of research and development of weapons (355.82) were moved here.

355.12068 Housing administration (355.67) was moved here.

355.342   Public relations (659.29355) was consolidated here.

355.43   Standard subdivisions of Nuclear operations were moved from 355.43001–.43009 to 355.4301–.4309.

355.52   Maneuvers involving civil populations (355.58) was merged here with Maneuvers.

355.6091   Treatment by areas, regions, places in general of Military administration is a new number.

355.614   Job descriptions for military personnel is a new number.

355.619   Civilian workers is a new number.

355.621   Supply administration now includes Administration of specific kinds of equipment and supplies (355.8), Supply management (355.8068), and Supply management of weapons (355.82068).

355.6212   Contracts (355.6211) is now found here with Procurement.

355.62132 Inventory control is a new number.

355.62137 Surplus supplies and their disposal is a new number.

355.68   Executive management is a new number.

355.685   Inspection (355.63) has been moved here under Executive management.

355.8   Comprehensive works on ordnance (355.82) were relocated here under Military equipment and supplies (Matériel) Weapons (Ordnance).

355.806   Organizations relating to weapons (355.8206) is now located here.

355.807   Education and related topics on weapons (355.8207) was moved here.

356.11   General topics of infantry (356.18) is now located here.

356.16   Motorized infantry (356.11) has been moved here under Troops having special combat functions.

357.185   Cavalry training (357.2) was consolidated here.

357.5   General topics of mechanized cavalry (357.58) was shifted here under Mechanized cavalry.

358.407   Air force research (358.40072) is now found here.

359.07   Naval forces research (359.0072) and comprehensive works on naval aspects of research and development of weapons (359.82) were merged here.

359.621   Naval administration now includes Administration of specific kinds of equipment and supplies (359.8) and Supply management (359.8068).

359.8   Comprehensive works on Naval ordnance (359.82) are now found here under Naval equipment and supplies (Naval matériel)   Naval Weapons (Naval ordnance).

The 360 division was pinpointed by a Comaromi survey as fourth among the 300 class needing revisions. The word *association* in the caption seems to puzzle users, although it is ignorance of the past that leads to the puzzlement. When one joins a group that has a purpose of some sort, one has *associated* himself or herself with it. The association is volitional, which is why such groups do not fall in 301–307.

Many people refer to the 360s as being applied sociology, which is a misnomer. Sociology cannot be applied any more than economics, political science, or the law can. Instead, except for associations, this division treats endemic and peculiar social problems.

Although the changes in the Summaries were minor, really just a shift in a word or two, there were many revisions hidden beneath. Insurance (368) underwent an extensive analysis and change to bring it up-to-date. Specific social problems and services in 362–363 have an updated Add Table, and there is a new Table for services to patients for specific conditions (362.196–.198). Standard subdivisions of Offenses against public health, safety and order were moved from 362.1400– to 364.140–.

Other changes follow:

361.06   Counseling (361.323) is now found here with guidance.

362   Comprehensive works on young men and women (362.7083)
           are now found here under Social welfare problems and services.

362.58   Interdisciplinary works on legal aid (347.017) are now found
           here under Remedial measures, services, forms of assistance.

362.7   Classes of young people (362.79) have been shifted here under
           Problems of and services to young people.

362.7083   Works on young people twelve to seventeen (362.796) have
           been moved here.

362.708691 Immigrants (362.799) are now found here under Persons with
           status defined by changes in residence.

362.7089   Young people twelve to seventeen (362.796) and Racial, ethnic,
           national groups (362.797) are consolidated here.

362.709   Urban and Rural youth (both 362.799) are now found at
           362.7091732 (Urban) and 362.7091734 (Rural).

363.1257   School traffic safety programs (371.7752) is now included here
           under Measures to prevent, protect against, limit effects of
           problems.

363.147   School athletic safety programs (371.7754) is now included
           here under Measures to prevent, protect against, limit effects of
           problems.

363.2068   Management of police services (351.74) is now found here.

363.379   Fire safety programs in schools (371.774) has moved here
           under Fire hazards in specific situations.

363.92   Population quality now includes Eugenic measures to control
           population (363.98).

366.1082   Women in Freemasonry (366.18) is now consolidated here.

366.1083   Young people of Freemasonry now includes the Order of
           DeMolay for Boys (366.17), found at 366.108351, and both
           International Order of Job's Daughters and International Order
           of the Rainbow for Girls (366.18) at 366.108352.

368.094   Comprehensive works on business insurance (368.81) have
           been consolidated here under Business insurance.

The structure of the 370s is so poor that a complete recasting of the division
was done early in the development of Edition 20 but shelved for a variety of reasons. This drive for renewing Education was resurrected in this edition, and much

of it was revised, especially 370.1, 370.7, 375–377, and 378.14–.19. Major changes include the relocation of 376 (Education of women) and 377 (Religious schools) to subdivisions under 371.

Several changes involve scattering aspects under subjects that were previously situated in one place. One such topic is Instructional facilities for teaching specific subjects (371.6234); Curricula and courses in bibliography, library and information sciences, and encyclopedias (375.01–.03) have been shifted to specific subjects in 010–039 and notation 071 from Table 1 added. Curricula and courses in knowledge, systems study, data processing, and computer science (375.04) have been shifted to 001–006 and notation 071 from Table 1 added. Curricula and courses of study in other specific subjects (375.05–.99) have been shifted to 050–999 and notation 071 from Table 1 added. The Summaries illustrate many of these changes.

Summary *(DDC 20)*		Summary *(DDC 21)*	
371	**School management; special education**	**371**	**Schools and their activities; special education**
376	**Education of women**	**376**	**Unused**
377	**Schools and religion**	**377**	**Unused**
379	**Government regular, control, support**	**379**	**Public policy issues in education**

Although all changes in 370 appear in the Comparative and Equivalence Tables in Volume 1, some are listed below.

371.042   Home schools and home schooling (649.68) are now located here.

371.07   Religious schools (377) have moved here.

371.223   Veterans' education benefits (362.8682) have been consolidated here under Scholarships and fellowships.

371.30281   Techniques for parents (649.68) has moved here under Techniques of study.

371.822   Education of women (376) is now found here.

372.4   Reading instruction in home schools (649.58) has been merged here under Reading.

378.32   Veterans' higher education benefits (362.8682) is now integrated here under Student aid.

The Summary of 380 shows no change from Edition 20, and indeed there are few modifications to the division, with just five listed below.

382.17   Relation of monetary conditions to world trade (382.174) has been shifted here under Balance of payments.

384	Interdisciplinary works on telecommunication (004.6) was consolidated here.
384.554	Public (noncommercial) television (384.55065) has been moved here under General broadcasting (Free television).
388.322	Comprehensive works on passenger bus services (388.3222) are now found here under Bus services.
389.109	Historical, geographic, persons treatment of Metrology (389.15) was moved here.

The Summary again would indicate little change in 390 (Customs, etiquette, folklore); however, it is deceiving for there have been quite a few changes, especially Holidays (394.26). If Custer's battle over moving Folk literature to other literatures failed, a small skirmish was won here with many revisions within Folk literature (398.2). A new Add Table has been developed. Treatment by specific locations and Tales from specific localities (398.21–.27) have been moved to 398.2093–.2099. Other changes found in the table include: Forecasting and forecasts (01) moved to 001; Statistics and illustrations (02) moved to 002; serial publications (05) moved to 005; and Museums (07) moved to 007.

390.0846	Persons in late adulthood of Customs, etiquette, folklore (392.9) are now located here.
394.26	Specific kinds of holidays (394.268), Seasonal holidays (394.2683), and Patriotic holidays (394.2684) are now consolidated here. Specific Patriotic holidays (394.2684) and Seasonal holidays (394.2683) are found in 394.261–.264.
394.265	Religious holidays (394.2682) are now found here.
394.266	Christian holidays (394.26828) have been moved here.
394.267	Jewish holidays (394.268296) have been moved here.
398	Special topics under folklore (398.04) are now found here.
398.09	History and criticism of folklore (398.042) have been consolidated here under Historical, geographic, persons treatment.
398.2	Comprehensive works on fairy tales (tales of paranatural beings) (398.21) are now found under Folk literature.
398.21	Witches (398.22) are now found here under Tales and lore of paranatural beings of human and semihuman form.
398.27	Comprehensive works on historical and quasi-historical events (398.22) are now found here under Tales and lore of everyday human life.

Exercises in the Use of Class 300

Here are twelve examples of books written about subjects found in the 300 class. From the summaries, develop classifications for each. Then, check them against the answers found in "Answers to the Exercises" in the appendix.

1. A work studying the effect that automobiles have had on American culture.
2. A work on the slave trade and slave ships in the seventeenth century.
3. A guide to financial planning.
4. A work on interracial conflicts, such as Black Korean, in American society.
5. A work on the wealthy in America.
6. A work on society's attitude and response to accusations of rape in American society.
7. A work on the power of the former Soviet Union's spy agency, the KGB, in modern Russia.
8. A work on the evolution of Chinese culture in the twentieth century as seen by a young Chinese woman, including reflections on her great aunt.
9. A work on the senior staff at the U.S. Department of Justice headquarters in Washington, D.C.
10. A work by an FBI agent who studies serial killers.
11. A work about four men who avenge their abusive imprisonment as children.
12. A work on using electronic resources for researching academic papers.

Literature Cited

Comaromi, John P. 1977. Decimal Classification Editorial Policy Committee report. *Library Resources & Technical Services* 21 (1): 94.

———. 1976. *The eighteen editions of the Dewey Decimal Classification.* Albany, NY: Forest Press Division, Lake Placid Education Foundation.

Class 400
Language

Introduction

John Phillip Comaromi, among others, long felt that fundamental changes in the way that DDC views language should be reviewed. A proposal was forwarded to the editor from an Editorial Policy Committee member to expand Grammar (—5) a great deal. Moreover, Comaromi had long felt that the composition of a language, up to the stage at which the composition moves into the literary (808), belonged in the usage of a particular language. Indeed, the underlying structure of DDC—with languages and literature separated by a chasm of science, technology, and the arts—continues to perplex many.

Outline and Details of Class 400

400	Language
410	Linguistics
420	English and Old English (Anglo-Saxon)
430	Germanic (Teutonic) languages German
440	Romance languages French
450	Italian, Sardinian, Dalmatian, Romanian, Rhaeto-Romanic languages
460	Spanish and Portuguese languages
470	Italic languages Latin
480	Hellenic languages Classical Greek
490	Other languages

Division 400:   The first division is used only for standard subdivisions (401–409) with the special topics bilingualism and multilingualism (404.2).

Division 410:   The second division is used for works on the structure of spoken and written language in general. The structure here is the same as in Table 4 and is followed by all of the succeeding languages: writing systems (—1 in Table 4, 411 in the Schedules); etymology (—2, 412); dictionaries (—3, 413); phonology and phonetics (—15, 414); grammar (—5, 415); slang, jargon, and the history or evolution of language (—7, 417); standard usage of language (—8, 418); and the last section is language other than that spoken and written, such as finger spelling (419), which is not duplicated in the divisions for specific languages.

Divisions
420–480:   The rest of the divisions are for specific languages, each of which is basically organized as is the 410 division. These are English and Old English (420); Germanic languages (430); French, Provençal, Franco-Provençal, and Catalan (440); Italian, Sardinian, Dalmatian, Romanian, and Rhaeto-Romanian languages (450); Spanish and Portuguese (460); Latin and Italic (470); and Greek (480).

Division 490:   The last division encompasses all other languages, which are East Indo-European and Celtic languages (491); Afro-Asiatic and Semitic languages (492); non-Semitic Afro-Asiatic languages (493), Altaic, Uralic, Hyperborean, Dravidian languages (494), languages of east and southeast Asia, Sino-Tibetan languages (495), African languages (496), North American native languages (497), South American native languages (498), and Non-Austronesian languages of Oceania, Austronesian languages, Esperanto and Interlingua (499).

The Number Building Process

Example 1.   A work on English to use in the business world.

The outline above and Relative Index indicate that English is found in 420. Reviewing the sections, we find the following:

421	**Writing system, phonology, phonetics of standard English**
422–423	**Etymology and dictionaries of standard English**
425	**Grammar of standard English**
427	**Historical and geographic variations, modern nongeographic variations**
428	**Standard English usage (Prescriptive linguistics) Applied linguistics**
429	**Old English (Anglo-Saxon)**

Because this work is about the *use* of English, the correct notation for this work would be that for Standard English usage.

428

Looking further under 428, we find the following:

Number built according to instructions under 420.1–428.

Looking under 420.1–428, we find the following:

Except for modifications shown under specific entries, add to base number 42 notation 01–8 from Table 4 ...

Referring to —8 in Table 4, we find the following:

—8	**Standard usage of the language (Prescriptive linguistics)** **Applied linguistics**
—81	**Words**
	Meaning, pronunciation, spelling
—82	**Structural approach to expression**
	Formal ... presentation of grammar, vocabulary ...
—83	**Audio-lingual approach to expression**
—84	**Reading**
—86	**Readers**

Because this work concerns the proper use of English, the appropriate notation should be —82, which, according to the instructions above, is added to 42 to get the following:

428.2

The next step is to bring in the aspect of business. To do this we go to Table 1 (Standard Subdivisions), where we find the following:

—024	The subject for persons in specific occupations
—024 09–024 9	Specific occupations
	Add to base number —024 notation 09–9 from Table 7 ...

Obviously, this work addresses the needs of office workers, both clerical and managerial. In the Table we find the following:

—65	**Persons occupied with managerial services**

Taking our 428.2, we add —024; then, as instructed, we add the —65.

428.202465   *Grammar for Business*

Example 2.   A work containing test questions on English as a second language.

We look once more at English. Referring to the instructions for 420.1–428, we turn immediately to Table 4. Again, —82 is the appropriate notation because it is a "formal ... presentation of grammar, vocabulary...."

428.2

Looking more closely under —82, we find the following:

—824   Structural approach to expression for those whose
                             native language is different ...

This is obviously the case in this classification, so we add 4 to our number.

428.24

Now we have notations for the language (English, 42) and the aspect of
learning the language by a non-English speaking person (—824). The next step is
to add the aspect of test questions. This would be a Standard subdivision, so it is
back to Table 1. We begin by looking at the Summary to lead us:

—01	Philosophy and theory
—02	Miscellany
—03	Dictionaries, encyclopedias, concordances
—04	Special topics
—05	Serial publications
—06	Organizations and management
—07	Education, research, related topics
—08	History and description with respect to kinds of persons
—09	Historical, geographic, persons treatment

This work is on learning English, so the obvious choice is —07.

428.2407

We are getting there, but this work is actually on tests for English as a second
language. When we look at the Summary for —07, we find the following:

—07 1–070 9	Geographic treatment
—071	Education
—072	Research; statistical methods
—074	Museums, collections, exhibits
—075	Museum activities and services Collecting
—076	Review and exercise
—077	Programmed texts
—078	Use of apparatus and equipment in study and teaching
—079	Competitions, festivals, awards, financial support

The obvious choice is —076, so we add 6 to our number.

428.24076   *Breaking the TOEFL Barrier*

DDC 21 Revisions

After the extensive revisions in Edition 20, Language has lain fallow through this
edition, for the most part. Class 400 and its associated Table (4) have very few changes.

Changes follow:

407.8	Language laboratories (371.6234) have been moved here.
410.151	Mathematical linguistics (401.51) is now found here under Mathematical principles.
410.285	Computational linguistics (402.85) has been relocated here under Data processing Computer applications.
419	Instruction in finger spelling (371.9127) is now consolidated here under Structured verbal language other than spoken and written.
419.071	Instruction in sign languages (371.9127) has been consolidated here.
439	Comprehensive works on Old Low Germanic languages (439.1) are now found here under Other Germanic (Teutonic) languages.
439.1	Yiddish (437.947) has been moved here under Other Germanic (Teutonic) languages.
439.2	Old Frisian (439.1) has been consolidated here under Frisian.
439.31	Old Low Franconian (439.1) has been merged here under Dutch.
439.4	Old Low German and Old Saxon (439.1) are now combined here under Low German (Plattdeutsch).
449	Langue d'oc (447.8) was consolidated here under Provençal (Langue d'oc), Franco-Provençal, Catalan.
491.49	Nuristani (Kafiri) (491.499) is now found here under Other Indo-Aryan (Indic) languages.
491.497	Romany (491.499) is now found here.
491.56	Dari (491.55) has been moved here.
491.57	Tajik (491.59) has been relocated here.
491.59	Pamir languages (491.593) are now located here under Other modern Iranian languages.
491.867	Moravian dialects (491.87) are now found here under variations of Czech.
492.79	Maltese (492.77) was moved here.
492.8	Argobba (492.877) is now located here under Ethiopian languages.
495.1	Beijing dialect (495.17) has been moved here under Chinese.

495.4   Himalayan languages, other than Kiranti (495.49), are now
located here under Tibeto-Burman languages   Tibetan.

Exercises in the Use of Class 400

Here are eight examples of books written about subjects found in the 400 class. From the summaries, develop classifications for each. Then, check them against the class numbers found in "Answers to the Exercises" in the appendix.

1. A work on the Portuguese language for English-speaking people.
2. A work on learning Russian.
3. A work on teaching yourself Swahili.
4. A dictionary of pronunciations of English language names.
5. A work on pronunciation of American English.
6. A dictionary of acronyms, initialisms, and abbreviations in the English language.
7. A French-English dictionary.
8. A Russian-English dictionary.

10

Class 500
Natural Sciences and Mathematics

Introduction

The word *science* contains the root of the word that means *"to know."* Knowing goes on throughout the Schedules; however, the ways of knowing differ from mode to mode, from reason to imagination to memory. The 500 class is nothing but a collection of topics that Western civilization has decided to call "science." The editors have correctly said that mathematics should not be a part of 500, thus it was renamed Natural Sciences and Mathematics in Edition 20.

The linear structure of the natural sciences in the DDC reflects the nature of the universe (from the broadest scale) to the nature of matter at the molecular level, which was the smallest known level in 1876; the nature of organic life at its earliest level on the planet (paleontology and paleozoology in 560) to its most recent and most highly developed level in the 590s.

Criticisms of the life science divisions have long been heard. More than thirty years ago, we were told:

> The science sections in the Dewey Classification ... with the emphasis on paleontology, fit American science in the later 19th century like a shoe. Unfortunately, the creature wearing the shoe turned out to be a millipede—a situation with which Dewey's successors were never able to cope (Richmond 1963, 399).

Outline and Details of Class 500

500	Natural sciences and mathematics
510	Mathematics
520	Astronomy and allied sciences
530	Physics
540	Chemistry and allied sciences
550	Earth sciences

560	Paleontology Paleozoology
570	Life sciences Biology
580	Plants
590	Animals

Division 500: The first division is used for general physical (500.2) and space sciences (500.5), and natural history (508). The standard subdivisions are also found here (501–507, 509), but History and description with respect to kinds of persons is separated from the rest (500.8).

Division 510: Mathematics is found in this division beginning with inductive and deductive mathematics, machine theory and similar aspects, graphs, combinatorial analysis, and mathematical models in the first section (511) followed by number theories and algebra (512); arithmetic (513); topology (514); calculus and other numerical analysis (515); geometry (516); and the last section is for probabilities (519.2); general game theory that is not associated with a specific application (519.3); the application of numerical analysis (519.4); sampling and statistics (519.5); programming (519.7); queuing and other applications of mathematics (519.8).

Division 520: Astronomy is located in this division in the sections 521 through 525. Gravitation, orbits, and similar topics are in the first section (521) and are followed by features usually found in the standard subdivision notation —028, which are techniques, procedures, apparatus, equipment, and materials (in this case, observatories, telescopes, and similar instruments). The next section is used for the universe, galaxies, and quasars (523.1); the solar system (523.2); our Moon (523.3); the planets in our solar system (523.4); meteors and solar wind (523.5); comets (523.6); our sun (523.7); stars (523.8); and natural satellites of other planets (523.9). Then in the usual egocentric way, our home, the Earth, is found in its own section (525). The next section is used for cartography, surveying, geodetic surveying, and geographical positions (526). Then locating, both in time and place, with celestial navigation (527), astronomical and nautical almanacs (528), and calendars (529) ends the division.

Division 530: This division is reserved for physics, and the first section contains the standard subdivisions (530.01–.09) plus general aspects of physics including relativity, quantum, and other theories (530.1); solid, liquid, gaseous states of matter in general (530.4); instruments (530.7); and measurement (530.8). The next three sections are used for more detailed works on the states of matter, which are dynamics, mass and gravity of matter, aspects of solid states, as well as energy in general (531); fluids and their properties (532); and the properties of gases (533). The next sections are for specific forms of energy, which include sound (534); light (535); heat (536); electricity (537); magnetism (538); and the last section is reserved for what is called "modern physics," which refers to the structure of matter (539.1); radiation (539.2); atoms and molecules (539.6); and atomic and nuclear physics (539.7).

Division 540: This section is used for chemistry (541–547), crystallography (548), and mineralogy (549). General topics of chemistry are in the first section, which are the standard subdivisions (540.1–.9), and like astronomy, chemistry begins with general aspects, which are physical and theoretical chemistry (541), then continues on to the features of Table 1 (—028), techniques, procedures, apparatus, equipment, materials (542). Specific branches of chemistry follow: analytical chemistry (543); qualitative analysis (544); quantitative analysis (545); inorganic chemistry, which encompasses specific elements and compounds (546); ending the chemistry sections with specific elements and compounds of organic chemistry (547).

Division 550: The division is reserved for the earth sciences of geology, hydrology, and meteorology (551), petrology (552), and geologic materials with economic value (553). The rest of the division (554–559) is used for geographic locations of the earth sciences.

Division 560: The seventh division is used for what euphemistically could be called the "old life" sciences of paleontology and paleozoology, which lead to the life sciences in the next division. The first section has the standard subdivisions (560.1–.9), and stratigraphic paleontology (560.17) and paleoecology (560.45). Paleobotany and fossil microorganisms are in the next section (561), then fossil invertebrates (562) followed by various fossil marine and seashore invertebrates (563); fossil mollusks (564); fossil arthropoda (565); fossil chordates (566); and continuing to move up the evolutionary chain we find fossil cold-blooded vertebrates and fishes (567); fossil birds (568); and lastly fossil mammals (569). Prehistoric man is found at the end of the division (569.9).

Division 570: This division is used for the life sciences with the standard subdivisions in the first section (570.1–.9) and microscopy (570.282) under Miscellany. Sections 571–575 are internal biological processes and structures, with the first two sections containing processes common to all organisms, which are physiology, diseases, reproduction, pathology (571), and biochemistry (572). Next are specific systems of animals and physiology (573) and the specific parts and systems of plants (575). The rest of the division is for more general aspects such as genetics and evolution (576); ecology (577); and adaptation, harmful or rare organisms, and organisms of specific environments (578). The next section begins with those devoted to the natural history of specific organisms, the first of which are microorganisms, fungi, and algae (579), which bridge into the last divisions.

Division 580: This division is used for books on the study of plants with standard subdivisions in the first section (580.1–.9), and genetics, evolution, adaptation, and plant ecology in the next section (581), which ends with the geographic treatment (581.9) in the second section. Next are herbaceous and woody plants noted for their flowers (582) followed by flowering plants (583–584); conifers (585); seedless plants (586); vascular seedless plants (587); and mosses and liverworts (588) concluding the division.

Division 590: The last division of the class is used for animals and is arranged like the division above. Standard subdivisions (590.1–.9) are first followed by genetics, evolution and the young of animals (591.3); adaptation (591.4); behavior (591.5); beneficial, harmful, rare, and endangered animals (591.6), animal ecology (591.7), and the familiar geographic locations of animals (591.9). Specific groups of animals finish the class beginning with invertebrates such as flatworms, roundworms, and other types of worms (592); salt-water invertebrates (593); mollusks (594); shrimps, mites, spiders, scorpions, centipedes, insects, and other arthropods (595); chordates (596); cold-blooded vertebrates such as fish (597); birds (598); and moving up the evolutionary chain to mammals (599), with humans at the top (599.9).

The Number Building Process

Example 1. A work on the blizzard of 1996 in New York State.

A good beginning shows *snow* classed in 551.5784 in the Relative Index. Checking the Schedules, we find that Meteorology is .5 under Earth sciences in 551.

.578 409	Historical and persons treatment
.578 41–.578 43	Properties, geographic distribution, variations over time
.578 46	Snow cover
.578 464	Ablation
.578 47	Snow formations
.578 48	Avalanches

Notations .57841–.57843 may be a possibility. Looking there we find the following:

Add to base number 551.5784 the numbers following 551.577 in 551.5771–551.5773 ...

Turning to 551.577, our choices are as follows:

.557 1	Properties
.557 2	Geographic distribution of precipitation
.557 3	Variations over time

None of these quite fit what the work is about, which is *snow storms*. Going back to the Relative Index, we find Storms:

Storms	551.55
meteorology	551.55
social services	363.349 2
weather forecasting	551.645
weather modification	551.685

It looks like the next stop in our voyage of discovery is 551.55. Although the other aspects were probably involved during the storm, the storm itself is the topic of this work.

.55	Atmospheric disturbances and formations
.551	Atmospheric formations
.552	Hurricanes
.553	Tornadoes
.554	Thermal convective storms
.555	Snow storms Including blizzards
.559	Other storms Including dust and ice storms

All of these categories involve unpleasant experiences, but at .555 we find blizzards under snow storms.

551.555

We now have the notation for the event and only need to add the location and time period. Looking under 551.555 we find no notation peculiarities indicated, so we return to 551.55 and find the following:

Standard subdivisions are added for atmospheric disturbances and formations together, for atmospheric disturbances alone

Obviously our next stop is Table 1 (Standard Subdivisions). We find in the Summary for —09 Historical, geographic, persons treatment:

—090 1–090 5   Historical periods
 ... Class historical periods in specific areas, regions, places in general in —091; class historical periods in specific continents, countries, localities in —093–099; class comprehensive works in —09

These instructions solved the problem of chronology, so we go directly to —093–099, where we find:

Add to base number —09 notation 3–9 from Table 2 ...

551.55509
Table 2 indicates that New York State is found at —747.

551.55509747   *Blizzard of '96, January 6–8, 1996*

Example 2.   A work on the ecology of rain forests in South America.

In the Relative Index, we find the following under Rain forests:

Rain forests	333.75
biology	578.734
ecology	577.34

The obvious number is 577.34.

577.34
Checking the Schedules, we find a "dagger" reference before Rain forest ecology, with the reference at the bottom of the page:

†Add as instructed under 577.3–577.6

The instructions given there are:

> 577.3–577.6   **Ecology of specific nonmarine environments**
> Add to each subdivision identified by † the numbers following
> 577 in 577.01–577.2 ...

Now turning back, we find that these are:

.01–.08	Standard subdivisions
.09	Historical, geographic, persons treatment
.1	**Specific ecosystem processes**
.2	**Specific factors affecting ecology**

Because there is no peculiarity for the locale notation (such as a specific number range) we turn to the standard subdivisions. This is not a specific place in South America; however, it is a specific continent. Thus, we should add to —09 the number from Table 2 for South America, which is 8.

577.34098   *The Land and Wildlife of South America*

DDC 21 Revisions

Natural sciences and mathematics have long been the focus of attention by both the Editorial Policy Committee and the editors. The last three editions have seen extensive revisions, and these endeavors have continued in this edition. The Summaries, however, do not give the revisions of this class justice.

Summary *(DDC 20)*		Summary *(DDC 21)*	
570	**Life sciences**	**570**	**Life sciences Biology**
580	**Botanical sciences**	**580**	**Plants**
590	**Zoological sciences**	**590**	**Animals**

Adding Biology to Life sciences, and the syntax change from the formal scientific terms Botanical and Zoological sciences to the more common Plants and Animals, seems to indicate stability in the class, but the reality is far from the appearance. Life sciences   Biology (570) is a completely new schedule that reuses numbers for different topics. Also, several new numbers were warranted by the advancement of knowledge. Revisions in the standard subdivisions and natural history (501–509) were few.

502.82   Simple microscopes (502.822) and Ultramicroscopes (502.824) are now found here under Microscopy.

508.2   This is a new number for Seasons.

Mathematics (510) was completely revised in Edition 18, but the result was not totally satisfactory to the users. Edition 19 included expansions, but again it was not found acceptable to all of the librarians using DDC. Edition 20 had some minor changes; the most effective were the relocations decimal numbering (to 513.55) and Business arithmetic (to 650.01513). Although the division Summaries display no changes, this edition contains many relocations, reductions, and new numbers within the sections and subdivisions.

511.52   This is a new number for tree graphs.

512.5   Algebras defined by dimension of space and other geometric algebras (512.53) is now found here under linear, multilineal, multidimensional algebras.

513.12   Separate and combined treatment of Arithmetic and algebra (513.122–.123) have been relocated here under Arithmetic and algebra.

513.13   Separate and combined treatment of Arithmetic and geometry (513.132–.133) have been relocated here under Arithmetic and geometry.

513.14   Separate and combined treatment of Arithmetic, algebra, geometry (513.142–.143) have been relocated here under Arithmetic, algebra, geometry.

514.3   Topological manifolds (514.233) is now consolidated here under Topology of spaces.

514.74   Global analysis and comprehensive works on global analysis (515) are now located here under Analytic topology.

514.742   This is a new number for Fractals.

515   Numerical analysis was added to this class.

515.38   Mixed equations (512.942) were moved here.

515.9   Abstract potential theory (515.7) is now found here under Functions of complex variables.

515.93   Riemann surfaces (515.223) was moved here under Functions of one complex variable.

515.94   Analytic spaces (Generalization of Riemann surfaces to n-dimensional spaces) (515.223) is now found here under Functions of several complex variables.

516   Constructive geometry (516.13) is now located here.

516.36   Local and intrinsic differential geometry (516.363) has been moved here under Differential and integral geometry.

519.2   Probabilities over rings, algebras, and other algebraic structures (519.26) has been moved here under Probabilities.

Although Astronomy and allied sciences entailed substantial changes in Edition 20, there were fewer and less substantial modifications in Edition 21.

520   Space (523.111) is now classed in 520.

522.68   Radar astronomy (522.684) has been shifted here under Nonoptical astronomy.

523.1126   Dark matter (523.1125) is now found here.

523.80216   Star catalogs (523.80212) were shifted here under Lists, inventories, catalogs.

523.841   Astrometric binaries (523.843) is now found here under Binary and multiple stars.

526.9   Land (boundary) surveying (526.92) has been moved here under Surveying.

527   Direction and course (527.5) are now located here under Celestial navigation.

The headings for Physics (530) as well as Chemistry and allied sciences (540) are essentially the same, yet there have been many modifications within the divisions. Many have been reductions, or the vacating of notations for particular subjects, which often have the consequence of the number being discontinued. One such example, Cavitation (533.295), under Vortex motion of gas dynamics, has been discontinued because there is no meaning in this setting. But in addition to eliminating notations, there have been expansions, such as Luminescence (535.35).

530.11	Conservation of mass-energy (531.62) is now located here under Relativity theory.
530.133	Bose-Einstein and Fermi-Dirac statistics (530.1332–.1334) are now found here under Quantum statistics.
530.1423	This is a new number for Supergravity.
530.444	Ionization of gases (530.43) has been consolidated here under Plasma physics.
530.801	Measurement theory (530.16) has been shifted here under Philosophy and theory of measurement.
530.81	Tabulated and related materials (530.8021 and 530.81021) are consolidated here under Physical units and constants.
531.16	Statics (531.162) are now found here under Particle mechanics.
531.55	Trajectories (531.31) was moved here under Projectiles.
532	Mass, density, specific gravity (532.04) is now located here under Fluid mechanics Liquid mechanics.
532.0595	Rotational flow (532.052) is now found here under Vortex motion.
532.595	Rotational flow under Hydrodynamics (532.51) has been merged here under Vortex motion.
532.597	Cavitation (532.0595 and 532.595) is now consolidated here.
533.295	Rotational flow (533.21) has been consolidated here under Vortex motion.
534.3	Frequency and pitch (534.32) are now found here under Characteristics of sound.
535.32	Rectilinear propagation (535.322) is now located here under Geometrical optics.
535.352	Fluorescence is a new number.
535.353	Phosphorescence is a new number.
535.355	Photoluminescence is a new number.
535.356	Thermoluminescence is a new number.
535.357	Electroluminescence is a new number.
535.52	Plane and rotary polarization (535.523–.524) are now found here under Polarization.
536.3	Reflection, refraction, radiation, absorption (536.31–.34) are now located here under Radiation.
536.4	Standard subdivisions of Effects of heat on matter were moved from .4001–.4009 to .401–.409.

536.44   Sublimation (536.445) is now located here under Vaporization and condensation.

536.50287   Resistance thermometry (536.53) is now found here under Testing and measurement of temperature.

537.1   Corpuscular theory (537.14) is now located here under Theories.

537.12   Specific wave theories (537.123–.125) are now found here under Wave theories.

537.24   Pyroelectricity (537.2442) is now located here under Dielectrics.

537.53   Thermionic emission (537.533) is now found here under Discharge through rarefied gases and vacuums.

537.6   Direct currents (537.61) are now located here under Electrodynamics (Electric currents) and thermoelectricity.

538.727   Paleomagnetic surveys (538.78) have been moved here under Paleomagnetism.

538.74   Pulsations (538.744) is now found here under Transient magnetism.

538.79   Observations of magnetic fields of solid earth at observatories (538.72) has been consolidated here under Magnetic observations at observatories.

539.736   This is a new number for Supercolliders.

539.76   Chain reactions (539.761) are now located here under High-energy physics.

541.224   Atomic bonds and interatomic forces (541.244–.246) are now found here under Chemical bonds, valences, radicals.

541.24   Spatial atomic arrangements (541.243) are now located here under Atomic structure.

542.1   Chemical laboratories (371.6234) has been moved here.

542.4   Blowpipes (542.5) are now found here under Heating and distilling.

544.95   Refractometric and interferometric analysis (544.953) is now located here under Optical methods.

545.4   Combustion and blowpipe analyses and Pyrolysis (545.42–.43) are now located here under Thermal analysis.

545.81   Refractometric and interferometric analysis (545.813) was now located here under Optical methods.

546.44   Standard subdivisions for Transuranium elements (.44001–.44009) are now found in .4401–.4409.

547.1223   Comprehensive works on stereochemistry (541.223) are now found here.

547.12252   Comprehensive works on isomers (541.2252) have been moved here under Physical and theoretical chemistry.

548.84   Cleavage, cohesion, density, specific gravity (548.843–.845) are now located here under Mechanical properties.

549.11   Minerals in placers (549.113) are now located here under Minerals in specific kinds of formations.

The inorganic and organic come together at the point where the "dead" Earth and the dead fossils found in the "dead" Earth coalesce. Paleontology and paleozoology are included under Life sciences (560–590) but act as a bridge to Earth sciences in 550. Once again, although the division headings for Earth sciences are basically the same, the division has received a great deal of attention resulting in extensive revisions, including many reductions and expansions in Atmosphere interactions with earth's surface, Faults and folds, and Semiprecious stones.

551.11   Gutenberg discontinuity (551.115) and Mohorovicic discontinuity (551.119) are now located here under the Interior of Gross structure and properties of the earth.

551.23   Volcanic volatiles (552.2) has been moved here under Thermal waters and gases.

551.38   Nivation (551.383) is now located here under Geologic work of frost.

551.43   Comprehensive works on slopes (551.436) are now located here under Elevations.

551.515   Statics and dynamics of the atmosphere (551.5152–.5153) are now found here under Dynamics.

551.524   Water temperature affecting atmosphere has been changed to Atmosphere interactions with earth's surface.

551.5246   Ocean and seas has become Ocean-atmosphere interactions. Specific oceans and seas have been added at .52463–.52467.

551.52509   Geographic distribution at earth's surface (Temperatures) (551.5252) is now found here under Historical, geographic, persons treatment of temperatures.

551.527   Corpuscular radiation (551.5276) is now located here under Radiations.

551.5409   Geographic distribution at earth's surface of Atmospheric pressure (551.542) is now found here under Historical, geographic, persons treatment.

551.55	Upper-atmosphere storms (551.557) are now located here under Atmospheric disturbances and formations.
551.563	Electricity of aerosols and dust (551.564) and Saint Elmo's fire (551.5633) are now shifted here under Atmospheric electricity.
551.571	Vertical distribution in troposphere and Humidity in upper atmosphere (551.5714–.5717) are now located here under Humidity.
551.57109	Geographic treatment in troposphere of humidity (551.5712) is now found here under Historical, geographic, persons treatment.
551.574	Condensations on objects in upper atmosphere (551.5747) are now located here under Condensation of moisture.
551.57846	Duration (551.578461) and Firnification and stratification (551.578465–.578466) are now located here under Snow cover.
551.5787	Formation of hailstones (551.5747) is now found here under Hail and graupel.
551.872	Faults is a new number.
551.875	Folds is a new number.
552.4	Serpentinites (552.58) has been consolidated here under Metamorphic rocks.
553.87	Jet (553.22) is now found here under Semiprecious stones.
553.873	Opals is a new number.
553.876	Jade is a new number.
553.879	Amber (553.29) has been moved here, a new number.

Life sciences (560–590) were among those that had such extensive changes that Comparative and Equivalence Tables are provided to DDC users. Only a few of the changes in these divisions are listed here—mainly, relocations of subjects from other divisions. The Summaries of Editions 20 and 21 display some of these modifications.

Summary *(DDC 20)*		Summary *(DDC 21)*	
561	**Paleobotany**	**561**	**Paleobotany; fossil microorganisms, fungi, algae**
563	**Fossil primitive phyla**	**563**	**Miscellaneous fossil marine and seashore invertebrates**
565	**Other fossil invertebrates**	**565**	**Fossil Arthropoda**
566	**Fossil Vertebrata (Fossil Craniata)**	**566**	**Fossil Chordata**
567	**Fossil cold-blooded vertebrates**	**567**	**Fossil cold-blooded vertebrates Fossil Pisces (fishes)**
568	**Fossil Aves (Fossil birds)**	**568**	**Fossil Aves (birds)**

Other changes follow:

569.9   Prehistoric humans, genus Homo (573.3), are now found here under Hominidae (Humans and their forebears).

The dissimilarities of the Summaries of 570 demonstrate the extent of the revisions. There is little resemblance between the two. Biological processes (571–575) and structures in plants and animals (580–590) are now part of this revamped schedule.

Summary *(DDC 20)*		Summary *(DDC 21)*	
571	**[Unused]**	**571**	**Physiology and related subjects**
572	**Human races**	**572**	**Biochemistry**
573	**Physical anthropology**	**573**	**Specific physiological systems in animals, regional histology and physiology**
574	**Biology**	**574**	**[Unused]**
575	**Evolution and genetics**	**575**	**Specific parts of and physiological systems in plants**
576	**Microbiology**	**576**	**Genetics and evolution**
577	**General nature of life**	**577**	**Ecology**
578	**Microscopy in biology**	**578**	**Natural history of organisms and related subjects**
579	**Collection and preservation**	**579**	**Microorganisms, fungi, algae**

Other changes follow:

579   Thallobionta (589) has been moved here under Microorganisms, fungi, algae.

579.3   Prokaryotes (Bacteria) was 589.9 but is now found here.

579.4   Protozoa (593.1) has been moved here.

Again, the Edition 21 Summary of 580 shows little resemblance to that of Edition 20. Sections 581, 583, and the subdivisions based on zeros are extensively revised.

Summary *(DDC 20)*		Summary *(DDC 21)*	
580	**Botanical sciences**	**580**	**Plants**
581	**Botany**	**581**	**Specific topics in natural history of plants**
582	**Spermatophyta (Seed-bearing plants)**	**582**	**Plants noted for specific vegetative characteristics and flowers**
583	**Dicotyledons**	**583**	**Magnoliopsida (Dicotyledons)**

584	Monocotyledons	584	Liliopsida (Monocotyledons)
585	Gymnospermae (Pinophyta)	585	Pinophyta (Gymnosperms) Coniferales (Conifers)
586	Cryptogamia (Seedless plants)	586	Cryptogamia (Seedless plants)
587	Pteridophyta (Vascular cryptogams)	587	Pteridophyta (Vascular seedless plants)
589	Thallobionta and Prokaryotae	589	[Unused]

Other changes follow:

580.282   Microscopy of plants (578) is now found here.

580.75   Collecting botanical specimens (579) has been shifted here under Museum activities and services, Collecting.

580.752   Preserving botanical specimens (579) is now found here.

The few changes seen in the Summaries belies the extent of the revisions in 590. Sections 591, 597, 599, and the subdivisions based on zeros are extensively revised.

	Summary *(DDC 20)*		Summary *(DDC 21)*
590	Zoological sciences	590	Animals
591	Zoology	591	Specific topics in natural history of animals
593	Protozoa, Echinodermata, related phyla	593	Miscellaneous marine and seashore invertebrates
595	Other invertebrates	595	Arthropoda
596	Vertebrata (Craniata, Vertebrates)	596	Chordata
597	Cold-blooded vertebrates; Fishes	597	Cold-blooded vertebrates Pisces (Fishes)

Other changes follow:

590.282   Microscopy of animals (578) has been repositioned here.

590.75   Collecting zoological specimens (579) has been shifted here under Museum activities and services   Collecting.

590.752   Preserving zoological specimens (579) is now found here.

591.5   Behavior (574.5) has been consolidated here.

591.562   Sexual selection (575.5) has been moved here under Sexual behavior.

599.9	Physical anthropology (573) has been moved here under Hominidae, Homo sapiens.
599.97	Human races (572) are now found here.
599.98	Specific races (human) has been shifted here from 572.8.

Exercises in the Use of Class 500

Below you will find ten summaries of books in the subject areas of Class 500. Apply your skills and develop classification numbers for each; then, check your numbers against class numbers in "Answers to the Exercises" in the appendix.

1. A work on earthquakes in geological perspective.
2. A work on the study and teaching of science in secondary schools in the United States.
3. A work on science fair projects in the fields of space flight and astronomy.
4. A work on the principles of scientific communication.
5. A work on the scientific explanations for the origin of Earth and its life forms.
6. A work on gorillas.
7. A serial on the behavior of animals living in Africa.
8. A work on plants in California.
9. A work on evolution from primitive forms of life.
10. A work on the history of the illustration of plants.

Literature Cited

Richmond, Phyllis A. 1963. The future of generalized systems of classification. *College and Research Libraries* 24 (5): 399.

Class 600
Technology and Applied Sciences

Introduction

The 600 class is one of the largest of all classes in number of entries and embodies the enormous growth of technology during the century since Dewey first developed his system. Only classes 610 and 620 were targeted for revision on the Comaromi survey, but they ranked second and third in the order of urgency. A major readjustment would move both Human anatomy (611) and Human physiology (612) into Zoology (591), partially to liberate space in the 610s and to affirm their relationship to the anatomy and physiology of animals. However, the idea was withdrawn after receiving extensive criticism.

Much like class 300, the problems of illogical arrangement, disciplinary overlap, and overcrowding in this class are widely recognized. According to one classifier, it is "an unpredictable disarray of 'disciplines' and/or subjects ... an arbitrary arrangement of a heterogeneous mass" (Kaltenbach 1968, 47).

What to do about these problems is less obvious. Recent questions from the field focus on increasing financial hazards attached to issuing new revisions:

> Is a new edition, on the lines with which we are familiar, probable? And
> if it is, do we want it? Well, I should think that on one plane (not the eco-
> nomic one, that is) we most certainly do. The classification has (as any
> classification will have) many areas where radical change is needed.
> Medical Sciences come at once to mind, and the Fine Arts.... In his re-
> cent review of DDC19 Peter Butcher has reminded us of the difficulties
> we experience with the 720/Architecture—624/Civil engineering—
> 690/Building split (A huge task, this, to rectify and rationalize this
> field—but one which should give great satisfaction when done). Life
> Sciences, 560, 70, 80, and 90 plus 611 and 612, stand greatly in need of
> rewriting (Jelinek 1980, 1–2).

If, when, and how such rewriting will be accomplished can be seen only as through a glass, very darkly. Meanwhile, 600 will remain a strange amalgamation of parts that are shoehorned together under the caption of Technology (Applied sciences).

Outline and Details of Class 600

600	Technology (Applied sciences)
610	Medical sciences Medicine
620	Engineering and allied operations
630	Agriculture and related technologies
640	Home economics and family living
650	Management and auxiliary services
660	Chemical engineering and related technologies
670	Manufacturing
680	Manufacture of products for specific uses
690	Buildings

Division 600: The first section is used for standard subdivisions, which are found in 601–609. Special topics (604) is used for technical drawing (604.2); methods used with hazardous materials (604.7); and history and description with respect to kinds of persons (604.8), which is usually —08. Including the subject here frees 608 to be used for Inventions and patents.

Division 610: Medicine is found in this division. Standard subdivisions (610.1–.9) are joined by nursing, which shares the notation for education and research (610.7), and other medical personnel are found with organizations and management (610.6). Human anatomy, cell and tissue biology are in the next section (611), followed by other general aspects of medicine such as human physiology (612); health education (613); medical jurisprudence and public preventive medicine (614); pharmacology, various types of therapy, and toxicology (615); and the various diseases (616). Wounds and injuries (617.1) are found in the next section with branches of medicine, including surgery and practices limited to certain regions of the body such as otorhinolaryngology (617.51); dentistry (617.6); ophthalmology (617.7); otology and audiology (617.8). The next to last section is used for the remaining branches of medicine including gynecology (618.1); obstetrics and childbirth (618.2–.8); pediatrics (618.92); and ending with geriatrics (618.97). Experimental medicine concludes the division (619).

Division 620: The third division is used for engineering and begins with standard subdivisions (620.001–.009) with the special topics of Engineering design, testing, and measurement and quality (620.004). Other general aspects of engineering are also in this section, such as the mechanics and materials of engineering (620.1); sound and similar vibrations (620.2); mechanical vibrations (620.3); engineering in certain environments (620.4); technology that works on the atomic or molecular level (620.5); concluding with ergonomics and safety engineering (620.8). The next section is used for engineering involving the principles of physics, such as energy (621.042); plasma (621.044); steam (621.1); hydraulics (621.2); electrical engineering (621.3); heat (621.402); vacuums and low temperatures (621.5); blowers, fans, and pumps (621.6); machine engineering (621.8); and ending with tools (621.9). Mining and ores are in the third section (622) followed by military and naval engineering (623); civil engineering (624); railroads and roads (625); hydraulic engineering (627); sanitary and environmental protection engineering (628). The final section of the division continues with other branches of engineering including aerospace (629.1); all types of land vehicles (629.2); vehicles that ride on cushions of air (629.3); astronautics (629.4); and concludes with automatic control engineering (629.8).

Division 630: Most of this division is reserved for Agriculture (630–636) and begins with the usual standard subdivisions (630.1–.9); however, specific techniques, apparatus, equipment, and materials that would normally be at 630.28 are in the next section (631) in order to provide sufficient room for the details required for agriculture. Plant damage by injury, disease, or pests is in the third section (632) followed by large scale plantings and crops (633); orchards, fruits (634.1–.8) and forestry (634.9); gardening and vegetables (635); and agriculture ends with animal husbandry (636). Processing dairy and poultry products (637) comes next followed by insect culture (638), which shifts from agriculture and agricultural products, followed by hunting (639.1); fishing (639.2); the culture of various aquatic animals (639.3–.8); and ending the division with conservation (639.9).

Division 640: Home economics and family care are in this division. The standard subdivisions are in the first section (640.1–.9) including special topics of household management (640.4). Food and drink are in the next section (641) followed by their consumption at meals (642). Aspects of managing households continue the division with housing and equipment used in it (643); utilities used (644); and furnishings used (645). Clothing, sewing, cleanliness, and guides to family living (646) begin a new group of subjects, which is followed by institutional housekeeping (647); housekeeping in the home (648); and the division concludes with child rearing (649.1–.7) and home care of the ill or disabled (649.8).

Division 650: This division is used for business office activities. Standard subdivisions are found first (650.01–.09), of course, with personal success in business (650.1). Office equipment, management, communication, and data processing are in the second section

(651) followed by methods used in written communication (652–653). Aspects of business accounting are in the next section (657) and is followed by management of the various activities such as the organization and its finance (658.1); production plants (658.2); personnel (658.3); top and middle management (658.4); production (658.5); materials (658.7); and marketing and distribution (658.8). Advertising and public relations conclude the division (659).

Division 660: Chemical engineering, metallurgy, and similar subjects are found in this division, which begins with standard subdivisions (660.01–.09), and includes biotechnology (660.6) and industrial stoichiometry (660.7). The production of chemicals used as raw materials or in the production of other materials is found in the second section (661) and is followed by the technologies for explosives and fuels (662). Commercial manufacture of beverages (663) and food (664) are next and are followed by the manufacture of waxes (665.1); fats and oils (665.2–.4); petroleum (665.5); and gases (665.7–.8). The various ceramic, masonry, and building materials are in the next section (666). Cleaning and coating of materials are next (667), which are followed by other organic-based products, such as plastics and perfumes (668), and metallurgy concludes the division (669).

Division 670: Manufacturing is in this division, and standard subdivisions in the first section (670.1–.9) are accompanied by factory operations engineering as a special topic (670.42). The Manufacture of products from specific materials are covered in the rest of the division, which are metal (671); iron and steel (672); nonferrous metals (673); lumber (674); leather and fur (675); pulp (676); textiles (677); rubber and similar materials (678); and other miscellaneous materials (679).

Division 680: This division is reserved for the manufacture of products for specific uses. There are no standard subdivisions for this division. The first section covers precision instruments (681.1–.4, .7); and printing, writing, and duplicating equipment (681.6); and ends with musical instruments (681.8). Blacksmithing comes next (682), then hardware and household appliances (683); furnishing and home workshops (684); leather and fur products (685); printing (686); and clothing (687). The manufacture of other items completes the division (688).

Division 690: Buildings are found in the last division of the class. Standard subdivisions are found in the first section, as usual (690.01–.09), with structural elements (690.1); general construction activities (690.2); and specific types of buildings (690.5–.8). Building materials are in the second section (691) and are followed by plans, drawings, and contracting activities (692). Types of materials used in construction are next (693–694). Aspects of the building process are found in the last sections of the class (695–698).

The Number Building Process

Example 1. A work on curing cancer using natural, dietary methods.

The Relative Index lists the following under Cancer:

Cancer (Human)	362.196 994
geriatrics	618.976 994
incidence	614.599 94
medicine	616.994
see Manual at 616.994 vs. 616.992	
nursing	610.736 98
pediatrics	618.929 94
social services	362.196 994
surgery	616.994 059

The work does not deal with any of the aspects but medicine, so we check the Manual as indicated and find the following:

Cancers vs. Tumors
... before using 616.992, check to be sure that benign tumors (616.993) are significantly represented. If in doubt, prefer 616.994.

Because the piece deals solely with the disease, cancer (.994), rather than tumors (.992) that may be benign (.993) *or* malignant, the appropriate notation is .994.

616.994
In the Schedules we find a "dagger" reference in front of Cancers, which directs the user to "†Add as instructed under 618.1–618.8."

When we look in the Schedules, we find "618.1–618.8 Gynecology and obstetrics." This branch of medicine is ignored, and the accompanying table is used for cancers of *all* types, not just gynecological and obstetrical. As we review the table, we find that the appropriate facet should be Therapy at —06.

616.99406
Now returning to the table, we have two choices of therapy, Drug therapy and Other therapies.

06	Therapy
061	Drug therapy
062–069	Other therapies
	Add to 06 the numbers following 615.8 in
	615.82–615.89 ...

Because this work is more or less about alternative, nonstandard therapies, the appropriate choice would be 062–069. Going on to the next step as instructed, we find at 615.8 Specific therapies and kinds of therapies.

.82	Physical therapies
.83	Therapies of light, heat, sound, climate, air, inhalation
.84	Radiotherapy and electrotherapy
.85	Miscellaneous therapies
.851	Mental and activity therapies
.852	Religious and psychic therapy
.853	Hydrotherapy and balneotherapy
.854	Diet therapy
	See Manual at 615.854
.856	Controversial and spurious therapies
.88	Empirical and historical remedies
.89	Other therapies
.892	Acupuncture
.899	Ancient and medieval remedies

Diet therapy at .854 looks like the appropriate choice, so we look up the reference in the Manual and find the following:

Use with caution; when a single food element is heavily emphasized, diet therapy may amount to drug therapy ...

This work deals with a wide selection of foods, and thus this warning does not apply. Taking 615.854 as instructed, we drop the 615.8, leaving 54, which is added to our numbers.

616.9940654   *How to Conquer Cancer, Naturally*

Example 2.   A work on the development of national agricultural research capacity in India.

The outline above shows that Agriculture is found in 630, which is the base number to use. Research is one of the standard subdivisions, and the Schedules indicate that the subdivisions appear in .1–.9. Referring to Table 1, we find research in 072.

630.72

Now, how do we add the locality, another subdivision? Checking under —072, we find the following:

—072 01–072 09   Geographic treatment of research and statistical methods together, of research alone
Add to base number —0720 notation 1–9 from Table 2 ...

In Table 2 we find that India's notation is —54.

630.72054   *The Development of National Agricultural Research Capacity: India's Experience with the Rockefeller Foundation and Its Significance for Africa*

DDC 21 Revisions

Even though major revisions requiring references in Comparative and Equivalence Tables have not been accomplished in 600, the editors were very busy upgrading many aspects of this class. The Summaries indicate little change in the headings beyond added inclusive phrases, such as *related*.

Summary *(DDC 20)*		Summary *(DDC 21)*	
630	Agriculture	630	Agriculture and related technologies
640	Home economics and services	640	Home economics and family living
660	Chemical engineering	660	Chemical engineering and related technologies
680	Manufacture for specific uses	680	Manufacture of products for specific uses

Within the divisions, many standard subdivisions have been shifted to accommodate the use of Tables. Most maintenance and repair aspects are now found in —0288 of the subjects. Interdisciplinary works on Waste technologies remain under 628.4, where they were moved in Edition 20; but specific subjects are now located under the subdivision —0286. Apparatus, equipment, materials of specific topics are now found in —0284.

Many aspects of Technology have been modified to correspond with those in 500 class. Several subdivisions of Hunting, fishing, conservation, and related technologies (639.37 and 639.5–.6) were adjusted to match those in 590, and Other Mammals (636.9) was revised to match revisions in 599.

Medical sciences   Medicine (610) is one of the largest of DDC divisions, and it supports what must be one of the largest bodies of literature available to libraries. The Summaries suggest the extensive changes that are found within the division.

Summary *(DDC 20)*		Summary *(DDC 21)*	
611	Human anatomy, cytology, histology	611	Human anatomy, cytology (cell biology), histology (tissue biology)
614	Incidence and prevention of disease	614	Forensic medicine, incidence of disease, public preventive medicine
617	Surgery and related medical specialties	617	Miscellaneous branches of medicine Surgery
618	Gynecology and other medical specialties	618	Other branches of medicine Gynecology and obstetrics

Other changes follow:

611.01816   Nucleic acids (612.01579) has been consolidated here under Physiological genetics.

612.014486   Cosmic rays (612.014487) are now found here under Particle radiations.

612.0145   Effects of sound and related vibrations, of radiations, of thermal forces, of electricity and magnetism (612.01454–.01457) are now found here under Extraterrestrial biophysics.

612.0154   Lipids, carbohydrates, proteins, pigments (612.01543–.01547) have been relocated here under Biosynthesis.

613.2   Beverages (613.3) and comprehensive works on nutritive values of beverages (641.2) have been moved here under Dietetics. Applied nutrition (641.1) has been consolidated here, also.

613.2082   Women under dietetics is a new number.

613.2083   Young people and Infants (616.20832) under dietetics are new numbers.

613.2085   Relatives, Parents and Mothers (616.20852) under dietetics are new numbers.

613.23   Calories under dietetics is a new number.

613.7148   T'ai chi ch'üan (796.8155) has been consolidated here.

616.079   Immunity has been expanded, with Interferons at .0791 and new numbers from .0796–.07997 for Immunogenetics.

616.0798   Antibodies (immunoglobulin) was 616.0793 but is now found here under B cells, a new number.

616.7   Nonsurgical aspects, as well as comprehensive works on orthopedics (617.3), are now found here under Diseases of musculoskeletal system.

616.8526   Food addiction (616.39808) has been consolidated here under Eating disorders.

616.8553   Agraphia (616.8552) has been consolidated here under Written language disorders.

616.8583   Homosexuality (616.85834) is now located here under Sexual disorders.

616.8584   Comprehensive works on compulsive behavior (616.85227) were moved here.

616.85841   Pathological gambling (616.85227) is now found here.

616.8900835	Young people aged twelve to twenty (616.89022) are now found here.
616.995	Pulmonary tuberculosis (616.99524) has been relocated here under Tuberculosis.
617.47	Orthopedic surgery of the musculoskeletal system (617.3) was moved here under Musculoskeletal system and integument.
617.5	Orthopedic regional medicine and Orthopedic regional surgery (both 617.3) were consolidated here under Regional medicine Regional surgery.
617.71909	Historical, geographic, persons treatment of Diseases of corneas and scleras (617.719009) has been shifted here.
617.9	Orthopedic appliances (617.307) was shifted here under Operative surgery and special fields of surgery.
617.95	Standard subdivisions of Cosmetic and restorative plastic surgery, etc. (617.95001–.95009), have been shifted to 617.9501–.9509.
618.2075	Diagnosis under obstetrics (618.22) was moved here.
618.31	Standard subdivisions of Extrauterine pregnancy (Ectopic pregnancy) are changed from 618.310– to 618.3100.
618.326	Standard subdivisions, microbiology, special topics, rehabilitation, special classes of diseases, preventive measures, surgery, therapy, pathology, psychosomatic medicine, case histories (.326001–.32609) are now found here under Diseases of specific systems and organs.
619	Experimental research on diseases (616.00724) has been moved here under experimental medicine.

The Engineering (620) Summaries indicate little change in the headings beyond the addition of "Environmental protection" to 628 (Sanitary and municipal engineering). The many new numbers, however, reflect advancements in the field since Edition 20. Changes include many reductions, which have moved aspects of a subject to the main number of the subject. Safety measures under Mine health and safety (622.8) have been split between 622.20289 for comprehensive works and Specific excavation techniques (622.22–.29) and the Table 1 notation —0289 added. Tests and measurements (629.1345) and Maintenance and repair (629.1346) of specific types of aircraft are now found under the type of aircraft (629.1332–.1333), with Table 1 notations —0287 (Tests and measurements) and —0288 (Maintenance and repair) added.

Other changes follow:

620.189   Miscellaneous rare metals (620.1899) are now located here under Other metals.

620.5   Nanotechnology is a new number.

621.16   Other stationary engines (621.166) are now located here under Stationary engines.

621.31933   Uninsulated wires (621.31932) are now found here under Wires.

621.35   Superconductivity is a new number.

621.3694   Nonlinear optics is a new number.

621.3821   Communications networks is also a new number.

621.3848   Stations and scanning patterns (621.38486–.38488) are now located here under Radar.

621.3886   Specific kinds of stations (621.38862–.38864) are now located here under Stations.

622.2   Comprehensive works on safety measures for excavation techniques (622.8) have been moved to 622.20289 and Comprehensive works on a specific excavation technique (622.8) have been moved to 622.22 through 622.29.

623.26   Land and water mines (623.262–.263) are now located here under Mine laying and clearance, demolition.

623.810287   Testing (623.819) is now found here with measurement.

624.0299   Estimates of labor, time, materials in Civil Engineering (624.1042) are now found here.

624.1   Special topics of Structural engineering and underground construction (624.104) are now located here under the base number.

624.10299   Estimates of labor, time, materials for structural engineering and underground construction (624.1042) are now located here.

624.2   Comprehensive works on construction (624.28) are now found here under the base number for Bridges.

624.20288   Maintenance and repair of bridges (624.28) has been moved here.

625.19   Models and miniatures of rolling stock for roads with two running rails (625.21–.26) are now found here.

625.7   Special topics of Roads (625.704) are now located here with roads.

625.70289	Safety measures of roads (625.7042) has been shifted here.
627.13	Earthwork (627.132) and Water supply of canals (627.134) are now located here under canals.
627.3	Port buildings (627.33) are now located here under Port facilities.
627.8	Metals dams (627.85) have been relocated here under Dams and reservoirs.
627.80284	Materials of dams and reservoirs (627.81) is now found here with Apparatus and equipment.
628.166	Defluoridation (628.1667) is now located here under Chemical treatment of the water supply.
628.167	Desalinization by freezing and use of gas hydrates (628.1675–.1676) are now located here under Desalinization.
628.1674	Electrodialysis (628.16742) and Piezodialysis (628.16746) have been consolidated here under Membrane processes.
628.1682	Countermeasures for detergent pollution of the water supply (628.16823) is now located here under Countermeasures for domestic wastes and sewage.
628.23	Ventilators of sewers (628.25) are now found here with Deodorization.
628.44	Special topics of Solid wastes (628.4404) are now located here under Solid wastes.
628.96	Pest control of Aquatic invertebrates (628.963), Molluscoids (628.964), and Cold-blooded vertebrates (628.967) are now consolidated here under Pest control.
628.969	Pest control of land carnivores (628.9697) is now located here under pest control of mammals.
629.1345	Measurements (629.13457) are now located here with Tests.
629.25	Parts and auxiliary systems of other kinds of power plants (629.259) have been relocated here under Engines.
629.442	Space laboratories (629.445) are now found here with Space stations.
629.454	Specific activities of Circumterrestrial and lunar flights (629.4542–.4545) are now located here under those flights.
629.455	Specific activities of Planetary flights (629.45502–.45505) are now located here under those flights.

Like Edition 20, there have been many modifications to 630 in Edition 21. As in the rest of the Technology class, many modifications have been reductions of aspects of a subject to the base number of the subject. Some division headings have also had some modifications.

Summary *(DDC 20)*	Summary *(DDC 21)*
630 **Agriculture**	**630** **Agriculture and related technologies**
631 **Techniques, equipment, materials**	**631** **Specific techniques; apparatus, equipment, materials**
635 **Garden crops (Horticulture)**	**635** **Garden crops (Horticulture) Vegetables**
639 **Hunting, fishing, conservation**	**639** **Hunting, fishing, conservation, related technologies**

The standard subdivisions of Field and plantation crops (633) are now .01–.09 rather than .001–.009. Many sections of 630 have undergone tremendous expansions. Groupings of plants by climatic factor (635.952); Care, maintenance, and training of livestock (636.083); Feeding livestock (636.084); Feeds and applied nutrition and Field-crop feeds (636.085–.086); Specific breeds or group of dogs (636.72–.75); and Other mammals (636.9) all have been expanded.

Many aspects of a section have been modified to reflect the numbers found in 500 Natural sciences. Hunting specific kinds of birds is notated by adding to 639.128, as a base, numbers found in Natural sciences under Aves, or Birds (598.3–.9). The culture of specific kinds of fishes (639.372–.377) have been relocated using the base number 639.37 and adding the number designations for the specific fish found in 500 Natural sciences under Fishes 597.2–.7.

Other changes follow:

631.52   Plant breeding (631.53) has been moved here under Production of propagational organisms and new varieties.

631.5233   Agricultural genetics is a newly assigned number.

631.875   Converted household garbage (631.877) is now found here under Compost.

632.3   Radiation injury (632.19), Pathological development (632.2), and Protozoan diseases (632.631) are now consolidated here under Diseases of plants.

632.5   The duplicate number for Weeds (632.58) has been eliminated.

632.95   Algicides (632.952) are now located here under Pesticides.

632.9517   Insecticides is a newly assigned number.

633.3   Comprehensive works on legumes (635.65) have been moved here with Legumes, forage crops other than grasses and legumes.

633.32   Trefoils (633.374) are now found here under Trifolium clovers.

633.366   Lotus (633.374) is now found here under Sweet clovers.

634.881   Soil working (634.81) has been moved here.

634.9565   Seeding at permanent site (634.9652) has been moved here under Propagation at permanent site.

634.974   Specific monocotyledons (634.9741–.9749) are now consolidated here under the base number.

635.9   Comprehensive works on groupings by means of propagation (635.94), Plant propagation from seeds (635.942), and Plants propagated by other means (635.946–.948) have been consolidated here under Flowers and ornamental plants.

635.9152   Nursery practice (635.969) is now found here.

635.91532   Propagating ornamental plants by specific means other than bulbs and tubers (635.94) is now located here.

635.94   The duplicate number for Plants propagated from bulbs and tubers (635.944) has been eliminated.

635.9523   Tropical plants under Groupings of plants by climatic factor is a new number.

635.9525   Succulent plants (635.955) is now found here under Desert plants, a new number.

635.9528   Alpine gardens (635.9672) is now found here under Alpine plants, a new number.

635.9678   Window-box gardens (635.965) has been moved here.

636   Interdisciplinary works on species of domestic mammals (599) have been shifted here under Animal husbandry.

636.0811   Animal shows and related awards (636.0079) and Show animals (636.0888) have been consolidated here under Showing.

636.082   Breeding stock (636.0881) have been moved here under Breeding.

636.0824   Specific methods of breeding (636.08241–.08243) have been relocated here under Breeding and reproduction methods.

636.0843   Feedlot management is a new number.

636.0845   Range management (636.01) has been moved here under Grazing, a new number.

636.085   Feeds and applied nutrition has new numbers for nutrients, from .08521–.08528.

636.0855   Specific feeds (636.087) are now found here under Feeds.

636.08556   Feed from wastes is a new number.

636.086   Green fodder (636.08551) and Dry fodder (636.08554) are now found here under Field-crop feeds.

636.0862   Silage (636.08552) has been moved here under Field-crop feeds, a new number.

Animals in Animal Husbandry:

636.0888   Hunting animals (636.0886) are now found here under Sport and stunt animals.

636.109   All breeds of Miniature horses (636.11–.17) are now consolidated here.

636.15   Comprehensive works on harness and draft horses (636.14) have been moved here under Draft horses.

636.16   Specific topics in animal husbandry of ponies (636.161) have been consolidated under the base number for Ponies.

636.175   Trotters (636.12) have been moved here under Standardbred horse.

636.4088   Swine for specific purposes other than food (636.41) are now found here.

636.5   Interdisciplinary works on species of domestic birds (598) are now found here under Poultry   Chickens.

636.69   Ratites raised for feathers (636.61) were moved here.

636.72   Nonsporting dogs have new numbers for Specific breeds or groups of dogs, from .728 through .7376.

636.82   Comprehensive works on Asian shorthair cats (636.825) and Other shorthair cats (636.826) are now consolidated here under Shorthair cats.

636.822   Manx cats (636.823) is now found here under Common shorthair cats.

636.824   Burmese cats (636.825) has been moved here.

636.9   There are new numbers under Other mammals for placental mammals .93–.98.

636.92   Marsupials (636.91) have been moved here.

636.929   Monotremes (636.91) have been moved here.

636.97   Animals raised for fur and fur farming (636.08844) have been consolidated here.

637.1   Comprehensive works on processing cow's milk (637.14) have been relocated here under Milk processing.

637.20287 Quality determinations of butter processing (637.22) are now consolidated here under Testing and measurement.

637.30287 Quality determinations of Cheese processing (637.32) are now consolidated here under Testing and measurement.

637.5	Chicken eggs (637.54), Fresh chicken eggs (637.541), and Eggs other than chicken eggs (637.59) have been consolidated here under Egg processing.
637.54	Dried eggs and their parts (637.543–.548) are now located here under Dried eggs.
638.1	Apiary establishment (638.11) has been relocated here under Bee keeping (Apiculture).
638.5	Resin- and dye-producing insects (638.3) are now included here under Other insects.

Animals in Hunting:

639.12	Hunting land birds (639.122) has been relocated here under Hunting birds.
639.12841	Hunting waterfowl (639.124) has been moved here under Specific kinds of birds.
639.31	Comprehensive works on fish culture in natural and artificial ponds (639.311) are now located here under Fish culture in fresh waters.
639.34	Comprehensive works on freshwater aquariums (639.344) have been relocated here under Fish culture in aquariums.
639.378	Amphibian farming (639.376) is now found here.
639.4	Other Bivalvia culture (639.4811) is now located here under Mollusk fisheries and culture.
639.46	Scallops (639.4811) are now located here.
639.5	Specific crustaceans other than decapods (639.54) are now located here under Crustacean fisheries.
639.54	The duplicate number for Lobsters and crayfishes culture (639.541) has been eliminated.
639.56–.58	Specific decapod crustaceans other than lobsters and crayfishes (639.542–.544) are now located here.
639.6	Crustacean culture (639.5) has been moved here.
639.7	The harvest and culture of Protozoa, Porifera, Cnidaria, Ctenophora, Echinodermata, and Hemichordata (639.73) are now located here under Harvest and culture of invertebrates other than mollusks and crustaceans.
639.75	The culture of specific kinds of worms (639.752–.758) have been relocated here under Worms.
639.9	Comprehensive works on the conservation of mammals (639.979) are now located here under Conservation of biological resources.

Cosmetic changes in the 640 Summary are indicative of the few changes in the divisions as a whole. However, there is now a comprehensive number for baked goods, 641.815.

Summary *(DDC 20)*		Summary *(DDC 21)*
646	**Sewing, clothing, personal living**	**646**	**Sewing, clothing, management of personal and family living**
647	**Management of public households**	**647**	**Management of public households (Institutional housekeeping)**
649	**Child rearing and home care of sick**	**649**	**Child rearing; home care of persons with illnesses and disabilities**

Other changes follow:

641.3   Mineral food (641.309) is now located here in Food.

641.552   Leftovers (641.6) are now found here under Money-saving cooking.

641.568   Cooking for Christmas (641.566) has been consolidated here under Cooking for special occasions.

641.58   Cooking with oil (641.583) is now located here under Cooking with specific fuels, appliances, utensils.

646.2   Comprehensive works on sewing for the home (646.21) are now found here under Sewing and related operations.

646.32   Comprehensive works on clothing for young adult men (646.308351) have been shifted here.

646.34   Comprehensive works on clothing for young adult women (646.308352) have been shifted here.

646.402   Comprehensive works on clothing for adult men (646.4008351) have been shifted here.

646.404   Comprehensive works on clothing for young adult women (646.4008352) have been shifted here.

646.724   Hairdressing (646.7242) and Hairstyling (646.7245) are now located here under Care of hair.

648.5   Dishwashing (648.56) is now located here under Housecleaning.

649.156   Upper classes (649.1562) has been relocated here under Children distinguished by social and economic levels, by level of cultural development.

649.1567   Migrant children (649.15675) are now located here under Socially and culturally disadvantaged children.

The Summary of 650 Management and auxiliary services has not changed from that in Edition 20, which is indicative of the few changes within the division. Other changes follow:

651.2   Standard subdivisions of Equipment and supplies of Office services have been moved from 651.2001–.2009 to 651.201–.209.

651.29   Materials of Office services (651.028) are now found here under Forms and supplies.

651.74   Standard subdivisions of Written communication were shifted from 651.74001–.74009 to 651.7401–.7409.

658.30081   Management of men (658.3042) has been consolidated here under Personnel management.

658.30082   Management of women (658.3042) has been consolidated here under Personnel management.

658.30083   Management of young people (658.3042) has been consolidated here under Personnel management.

658.30084   Management of personnel in specific stages of adulthood (658.3042) has been consolidated here under Personnel management.

658.30087   Management of personnel with disabilities and illnesses, gifted persons (658.3045), has been moved here.

658.30089   Management of personnel belonging to nondominant racial, ethnic, or national groups (658.3041) has been moved here.

658.312408   Training of specific kinds of employees other than those occupying specific types of positions (658.31245) is now consolidated here.

658.325   Benefits not provided for elsewhere (658.3254) are now located here under Employee benefits.

658.54   Comprehensive works on work studies (658.542) are now found here under Work studies.

658.83408   Consumer research with specific types of consumers (658.8348) is now found here.

The Summaries suggest more changes in 660 Chemical engineering than have occurred. Modifications are of the minor cleanup kind.

Summary *(DDC 20)*		Summary *(DDC 21)*	
660	**Chemical engineering**	**660**	**Chemical engineering and related technologies**
661	**Industrial chemicals technology**	**661**	**Technology of industrial chemicals**
662	**Explosives, fuels technology**	**662**	**Technology of explosives, fuels, related products**
665	**Industrial oils, fats, waxes, gases**	**665**	**Technology of industrial oils, fats, waxes, gases**
667	**Cleaning, color, related technologies**	**667**	**Cleaning, color, coating, related technologies**

However, one significant change involves Methods of applying a specific kind of coating (667.9), which are now found with the kind of coating, such as painting.

Other changes follow:

660.65	Genetic engineering (575.10724) has been consolidated here under Biotechnology.
664.00286	Waste technology (664.096) has been moved here.
664.09	The duplicate number for packaging (664.092) has been eliminated.
664.1028	Auxiliary techniques and procedures under Sugars, syrups, their derived products (664.11) have been moved here.
664.10284	Apparatus and equipment under Sugars, syrups, their derived products (664.11) have been moved here.
664.10286	Waste technology under Sugars, syrups, their derived products (664.119) has been moved here.
664.36	Other salad and cooking oil (664.369) is now located here under Salad and cooking oils.
664.368	Soy oil (664.369) is now located here.
664.72	Other cereal grains (664.725) is now located here under Milling and milling products.
664.724	Corn for milling (664.725) has been moved here.
668.92	Polymerization (660.28448) is now found here.
669.141	Other iron alloy practices (669.1419) are now located here under Production of iron.

Modifications of 670 Manufacturing, 680 Manufacture for specific uses, and 690 Buildings were not only minor, but few in number. However, the Summaries did show the few changes seen below.

Summary *(DDC 20)*		Summary *(DDC 21)*	
671	Metalworking and metal products	671	Metalworking processes and primary metal products
680	Manufacture for specific uses	680	Manufacture of products for specific uses
687	Clothing	687	Clothing and accessories
693	Specific materials and purposes	693	Construction in specific types of materials and for specific purposes

Other changes follow:

671.52   Flow welding (671.529) is now located here under Welding.

673   Rare-earth and actinide-series metals (673.29) are now located here under Nonferrous metals.

673.7   Mercury (673.71), Antimony, arsenic, bismuth (673.75), and Miscellaneous rare metals and metalloids (673.79) are now consolidated here under Other nonferrous metals.

673.72   Alkali and alkaline-earth metals (673.725) are now located here under Light, alkali, alkaline-earth metals.

677.0028   Auxiliary techniques and procedures (677.028) is now located here.

681.25   Polarimeters (681.416) and Optical testing, measuring, sensing instruments (681.4) have been moved here.

681.761   Artificial legs and crutches (685.38) are now found here under Medical equipment.

697.07   Heating apparatus (697.0028) has been consolidated here under Heating equipment.

697.507   Steam heating apparatus (697.50028) has been consolidated here under equipment.

697.933   Unitary and combination systems (697.934) is now found here under Air-conditioning systems.

698.1028   Maintenance and repair of detail finishing (698.10288) is now located here under Auxiliary techniques, etc.

Exercises in the Use of Class 600

Now you can try your hand at classifying in the 600 class using these eight summaries of published books. Check your numbers against the class numbers in the "Answers to the Exercises" section in the appendix.

1. A work on how to seem to be in control at the office.
2. A veterinarian's dog stories.
3. A popular guide to woman-man relations.
4. A work about sleep.
5. A work on diseases due to tropical climates.
6. A work on wines from southwest France.
7. A work on migraines.
8. A work on modern technology and production.

Literature Cited

Jelinek, Marjorie. 1980. Twentieth Dewey: An exercise in prophecy. *Catalogue Index* 58: 1–2.

Kaltenbach, Margaret. 1968. Problems associated with presenting and teaching the schedules: Science (500) and Technology (600). In *The Dewey Decimal Classification: Outlines and papers presented at a workshop on the teaching of classification.* New York: School of Library Science, Columbia University.

ΙΙΙΙ 12

Class 700
The Arts
Fine and Decorative Arts

Introduction

The Dewey Decimal Classification is used successfully by several large art libraries, although it is designed primarily as a comprehensive scheme for general collections. A well-known art librarian says:

> While other approaches to classification systems have been pioneered by art librarians in the United States and abroad, e.g., the faceted classification for fine arts devised by Peter Broxis and special systems prepared by other English art librarians, most art libraries in the United States use the Dewey decimal classification system (DDC) or the Library of Congress system (LC), or systems modified from the Dewey or LC systems. For example, the systems used in the libraries of the Metropolitan Museum of Art and the Art Institute of Chicago are derived from the notation principles used in Dewey....
>
> Dewey remains a popular system in American libraries, and may be satisfactory in smaller art library collections where close classification is not considered an important factor.
>
> Neither system may be as successful as faceted classification systems in analysing complex works. However, as Wolfgang Freitag has observed: "A detailed enumerative system, in spite of all its errors and shortcomings, will meet the practical requirements of libraries far better than the few principles and guidelines provided in a system of faceted classification" (Walker 1975, 452, 469).

The entire 700 class has been faulted for its fragmentation and overlapping, but criticisms tend to focus on the final two divisions (Hickey 1968, 34).

Note that by "arts" is not meant the medical arts, the engineering arts, the agricultural arts, the domestic arts, the management arts, the industrial arts, or the building arts; but landscaping arts, architectural (building) arts, carving arts, arts in two dimensions, the photographic arts (even if highly technical as in the making of motion pictures), and the athletic arts are meant. You can see easily enough, we believe, that "art" has no meaning in the DDC.

Outline and Details of Class 700

700	The arts Fine and decorative arts
710	Civil and landscape art
720	Architecture
730	Plastic arts Sculpture
740	Drawing and decorative arts
750	Painting and paintings
760	Graphic arts Printmaking and prints
770	Photography and photographs
780	Music
790	Recreational and performing arts

Division 700: The first division is used for two separate standard subdivisions: the first (700.1–.9) is used for the arts in general, or to use when more than one type of art is discussed, and the other (701–708) is used for fine arts, decorative arts, and iconography. Unusual notations are History and description with respect to kinds of persons used in place of special topics (704), which leaves 708 for Galleries, museums, and private collections of fine and decorative arts. Impermanent collections and exhibits are separate in notation 707.4 under education and research. Iconography is in 704.9.

Division 710: Area planning is in the first section of this division (711) and the rest are devoted to landscaping. Landscape design is first (712), which is followed by landscape of roads (713). The next four sections cover specific elements of landscape architecture, which are water, (714), woody plants (715), herbaceous plants (716), and structures (717). The division finishes with landscape design of cemeteries (718) and natural landscapes (719).

Division 720: The third division is reserved for architecture, which encompasses architectural structure (721) and historical examples (722–724). The next four sections are used for buildings organized by their use, which are public (725), religious (726), education and research (727), and residential (728). The last section deals with the accessories or decorations of structures (729).

Division 730: Sculpture is in the next division, which has its standard subdivisions alone in the first section (730.1–.9), then it continues through 735 beginning with materials, equipment, techniques, and forms of sculpture (731), then historical styles of sculpture conclude the subject (732–735). Related arts are found in 736–739 with the standard subdivisions for them in the first section (730.01–.09). The first of these arts is carving (736), which is followed by numismatics and sigillography (737), ceramics (738), and ending with artistic metalwork (739).

Division 740: Drawing is in the first three sections with various types of decorative art, which complete the division. There are no standard subdivisions for the division as a whole, but many subjects begin with their own distinctive standard subdivisions. The first section is used for drawing (741), followed by aspects of drawing, which are perspective (742) and drawings organized by subject (743). Antiques, the design of mass-produced items, the design of objects arraigned historically, handicrafts, calligraphy, the design of heralds, decorative coatings, dioramas and similar displays, and floral arrangements are found in the next section (745). These are followed by weaving, lace-making, tapestries, needlework and embroideries, textile dyeing and printing, fashion design, rugs and other household furnishings made of textiles (746). Interior decorating (747), various decorative uses of glass (748), and furniture and picture frames conclude the division (749).

Division 750: Painting is found in this division, and its standard subdivisions are in the first section (750.1–.8); however, the historical, geographic, persons treatment (759) and techniques, procedures, apparatus, equipment, materials and forms (751), which would usually be with the other standard subdivisions, are in their own sections to allow enough notations for their complexities. The aspect of color in painting is found in the third section (752) and is followed by iconography, which is found in the next five sections beginning with symbolism and similar subjects (753), genre paintings (754), and religion (755). Then follow subjects of paintings (757–758), historical, geographic, persons treatment of painting to conclude the division (759).

Division 760: Graphic arts and methods of making prints are in this division with standard subdivisions and special topics of graphic arts in the first section (760.01–.09) and standard subdivisions for printmaking (760.1–.8). Sections 761–767 are used for various methods of printmaking, and prints are in 769.

Division 770: This division is used for photography with its standard subdivisions in the first section (770.1–.9) except for techniques, procedures, apparatus, equipment, and materials, which are in their own section (771), followed by photographic processes in 772–774. Special kinds of photography, cinematography, video production, and similar activities are found next (778). Photographs conclude the division (779).

Division 780:   Music, its standard subdivisions (780.1–.9), and its relation to other subjects (780.0001–.0999) are in the first section. The general principles of music and forms or kinds of music are next (781), followed by vocal music (782), and music for single voices and books on other aspects of the musical voice (783). Instrumental music concludes the divisions (784–788). As an option, composers and traditions of music may be classed in 789, which is not regularly used, rather than in 780–788.

Division 790:   Recreation and performing arts are covered in the last division, beginning with standard subdivisions of recreation (790.01–.09), with recreational activities (790.1) and the general aspects of performing arts (790.2) in the first section. Public performances such as traveling shows (791.1), circuses (791.2), motion pictures (791.43), radio (791.44), television (791.45), puppet shows (791.5), pageants (791.6), and animal shows (791.8) are in the second section and are followed by stage presentations (792). Games are in the next divisions, which are indoor amusements (793), indoor games of skill (794), games of chance (795), and athletic and outdoor sports (796–797). Recreation ends with fishing, hunting, and shooting (799).

The Number Building Process

Example 1.   A work on shade and urban forestry.

We find both Forests and Forest lands in the Relative Index in 333.75, which we then find in the Schedules:

Class here national forests; jungles, rain forests, woodlands;
old-growth forest; timber resources.

Not quite what we want. Forestry is listed as follows:

Forestry   634.9
    public administration   354.55

This work is not at all about public administration, so we next look under Forestry 634.9. The Summary lists:

634.92   **Forest management**
    .93   **Access and safety features**
    .95   **Silviculture**
    .96   **Injuries, diseases, pests**
    .97   **Kinds of trees**
    .98   **Forest exploitation and products**
    .99   **Agroforestry**

None of these apply to the work in question, so let's turn to the urban environment as the key to this work. The Relative Index has Urban forestry classed in 635.977, where we find the following:

.977 Trees
      Class here urban forestry; potted, shade, street trees

This looks like it may be an appropriate notation until we review the work again and find that it is more about trees and shade in landscape design than forestry. The Relative Index shows Landscape architecture and Landscape design in 712; however, this is more Landscape architecture in general, and this book is about trees specifically. Looking through the specific elements in Landscape architecture, we find Woody plants in landscape architecture in 715, with Trees at .2.

715.2
Now for the location indicator. There are no peculiarities for standard subdivisions mentioned in the section, so we turn to the Tables. Table 1 indicates that Treatment by areas, regions, places in general are found in —091. Under that notation we find the following:

Add to base number —091 the numbers following —1 in notation 11–19 from Table 2 ...

In Table 2 we find Urban regions at —173 2. According to instruction, we add 091, then 732.

715.2091732 *Shading Our Cities: A Resource Guide for Urban and Community Forests*

Example 2. A collection of U.S. Civil War photographs.

The Relative Index indicates that photographs are found in 779.

779
Under 779 we find the following:

Add to base number 779 the numbers following 704.94 in 704.942–704.949 ...

Going to the next step, we find specific subjects in 704.942–.949.

704.942	**Human figures**
.943	**Nature and still life**
.944	**Architectural subjects and cityscapes**
.946	**Symbolism and allegory**
.947	**Mythology and legend**
.948	**Religion**
.949	**Other specific subjects**

At 704.949 Other specific subjects we find:

Add to base number 704.949 notation 001–999 ...

It looks like the U.S. Civil War will be in .949. In the Relative Index we find the notation 973.7 for the Civil War. Following the directions, we add this to the base number 704.949 to get 704.9499737.

Now, according to the instructions under 779, we take the numbers following 704.94 (99737) and add them to 779.

779.99737   *The Civil War*

DDC 21 Revisions

The extensive changes found in Edition 20, especially that of the recasting of Music (780), which delayed the planned revisions of Education and Life sciences to this edition, still left more work to be done in Edition 21. The Summaries show only one minor modification in the 700 heading.

Summary *(DDC 20)*	Summary *(DDC 21)*
700 The arts	**700 The arts Fine and decorative arts**

Many new numbers have been added, mostly in Recreational and performing arts; however, music includes three new types of music. Other changes include those resulting from applications or alterations of Tables. Table 1 is now applied in the following topics: Auxiliary techniques and procedures in —28; Routine maintenance and repair in —288; and Safety measures in —289.

The 721–729 table for Specific aspects of architecture has been altered: Routine maintenance and repair (0289) is now under 0288 with Maintenance and repair; Architecture with respect to kinds of persons such as with disabilities (042), in late adulthood (043), and with illnesses (043) are now found here under 08 (087, 0846, and 0877, respectively).

The table for Textile arts (746) has undergone some revisions: Conservation, preservation, restoration (0488) is now found under 0288; Costume (746.92) under 0432; Pictures, hangings, tapestries (746.3) are now 0433; and Interior furnishings (746.94–.98) are 0434–0438. Finally, in Textile products and processes (746.1–.9), the preferred order now puts the process before the product.

Many of the section headings have been altered to reference more specifically the subject (e.g., "Water features" added "in landscape architecture") or to be more inclusive (e.g., "Sculpture to ca. 500" has become "Sculpture from earliest times to ca. 500, sculpture of nonliterate peoples"). The following Summaries list the changes in the section headings.

Summary *(DDC 20)*		Summary *(DDC 21)*	
712	Landscape architecture	712	Landscape architecture (Landscape design)
714	Water features	714	Water features in landscape architecture
715	Woody plants	715	Woody plants in landscape architecture
716	Herbaceous plants	716	Herbaceous plants in landscape architecture
717	Structures	717	Structures in landscape architecture
722	Architecture to ca. 300	722	Architecture from earliest times to ca. 300
726	Buildings for religious purposes	726	Buildings for religious and related purposes
727	Buildings for education and research	727	Buildings for educational and research purposes
729	Design and decoration	729	Design and decoration of structures and accessories
732	Sculpture to ca. 500	732	Sculpture from earliest times to ca. 500, sculpture of nonliterate peoples
742	Perspective	742	Perspective in drawing
751	Techniques, equipment, forms	751	Techniques, procedures, apparatus, equipment, materials, forms
755	Religion and religious symbolism	755	Religion
757	Human figures and their parts	757	Human figures
759	Historical, areas, persons treatment	759	Historical, geographic, persons treatment
766	Mezzotinting and related processes	766	Mezzotinting, aquatinting, related processes
771	Techniques, equipment, materials	771	Techniques, procedures, apparatus, equipment, materials
778	Fields and kinds of photography	778	Specific fields and special kinds of photography; cinematography and video production; related activities
784	Instruments and instrumental ensembles	784	Instruments and instrumental ensembles and their music
785	Chamber music	785	Ensembles with only one instrument per part

| 786 | Keyboard and other instruments | 786 | Keyboard, mechanical, electrophonic, percussion instruments |
| 787 | Stringed instruments (Chordophones) | 787 | Stringed instruments (Chordophones)   Bowed stringed instruments |

Other changes follow:

702.88   Routine maintenance and repair (702.89) is now found here under Maintenance and repair.

715   Comprehensive works on plants in landscape architecture (712) are now found here under Woody plants in landscape architecture.

720.846   Architecture for persons in late adulthood (720.43) was relocated here.

720.87   Architecture for persons with disabilities (720.42) was shifted here.

720.877   Architecture for persons with illnesses (720.43) is now found here.

720.9460902   Mudéjar architecture (723.3) was consolidated here.

727   Design of educational buildings for noninstructional objectives (371.629) has been moved here.

731.4   Comprehensive works on techniques, procedures, apparatus, equipment, materials together (731.028) are now located here.

741.0288   Conservation, preservation, restoration of Drawing and drawings (741.218) and their routine maintenance and repair (741.219) are now found here.

751.6   Routine maintenance and repair of paintings (751.67) are now located here under Maintenance and repair.

759.9   Soviet Central Asia under Geographic treatment of Painting and paintings has been moved to 759.9584–.9587 from 759.7.

769.0288   Conservation, preservation, restoration of prints (769.18) is now found here with Maintenance and repair.

774.0153   Physical principles of Holography (535.4) has been consolidated here.

778.55   Projection of specific kinds of motion pictures (778.554) is now located here under Motion picture projection.

778.59   Video production has been expanded, with new numbers from .590288 through .598.

781.645   Ragtime is a new number.

781.646   Reggae is a new number.

781.649   Rap is a new number.

790.2088375   Public entertainment activities of students (371.89) is now found here.

792.78   Theatrical dancing (792.8) has been moved here.

793.85   Card tricks (795.438) are now found here.

796   Activities and programs for families (796.0191) are now located here with Athletic and outdoor sports and games.

796.042   Intramural sports (371.89) was moved here.

796.068   Physical education facilities (371.624) was moved here.

796.08   Activities and programs for specific classes of persons (796.019) is now found here under History and description of sports and games with respect to kinds of persons.

796.156   Model racing cars (790.133) have been moved here.

796.22   Skateboarding (796.21) is now found here.

796.332028   Auxiliary techniques and procedures (796.3322) of American football is now located here.

796.4257   Triathlon is a new number.

796.58   Orienteering (796.51) has been moved here.

796.63   Mountain biking is a new number.

796.964   Curling is a new number.

797.1224   Kayaking is a new number.

798.83   Sled dog racing is a new number.

799.2   Comprehensive works on commercial and sports hunting (639.1) were moved here.

799.244   Hunting of specific waterfowl (799.24841) is now included here under waterfowl.

799.246   Hunting of Upland game birds (799.242) and Galliformes (799.24861) are now found here.

799.24833   Comprehensive works on shore and bay bird hunting (799.243) have been moved here.

Exercises in the Use of Class 700

Using class 700 and the Tables, assign classification numbers to the following books; then, check your classifications against the class numbers in the "Answers to the Exercises" section in the appendix.

1. An autobiography by a basketball player.
2. A work on the history of American art.
3. A work on American country music.
4. A work on a supercomputer programmed to play chess.
5. A work on Californian architecture.
6. A work on a Los Angeles, California, art museum's collection.
7. A biography of a modern architect.
8. A work on the history of art in the San Francisco area.
9. A work on African American art.
10. A work on a modern landscape architect.
11. A work on four screenplays.

Literature Cited

Hickey, Doralyn J. 1968. Problems associated with presenting and teaching the Schedules: Philosophy (100); Religion (200); and the Fine Arts (700). In *The Dewey Decimal Classification: Outlines and papers presented at a workshop on the teaching of classification.* New York: School of Library Science, Columbia University.

Walker, William B. 1975. Art books and periodicals: Dewey and LC. *Library Trends* 23 (3): 452, 469.

||||| 13

Class 800
Literature (Belles-Lettres)
and Rhetoric

Introduction

We have been told that Dewey's early contributions to the principle of faceting were evident in language (the 400s), literature (the 800s), and history/geography (the 900s) (Batty 1976, 212). Class 800 intricacies multiplied through the years, showing substantive changes, particularly in its auxiliary tables, and instructional changes in the schedules. Most criticisms address its formal presentation rather than its content. However, a critique of its assumptions concerning literary forms appeared at the time *DDC 18* was published.

The most common problems are the following.

1. Problems encountered by the catalogers:
    (a) the difficulty in application caused by the lack of clear, workable definitions of the forms;
    (b) the problems of treating works of mixed forms or uncertain forms; and
    (c) some of the forms that are questionable in their nature as literary forms.

2. Problems encountered by the users:
    (a) inconvenience resulting from the separation and scattering of works written by and about single authors; and
    (b) confusion caused by the seemingly arbitrary decisions made by the catalogers as regards the forms of certain literary works (Chan 1971, 458).

Bloomberg and Weber give special attention to the analysis of long DDC class 800 numbers.

This approach is most appropriate in this class because of the many different possible subdivisions and elements represented in each number. These elements include the base number for the language, a possible number for literary form (poetry or drama, for example), a possible number for the time or period of the work, a number for collections or history and criticism, and, finally, a number for specific themes (Bloomberg and Weber 1976, 151).

Table 3 (Subdivisions of Individual Literatures) made its first appearance in *DDC 18* (1971). Not surprisingly, it proved hard to apply, although it was a move toward synthetic faceting.

> In theory, synthesizing a literature number was quite simple. The classifier found a base number for a literature from the Schedules, turned to Table 3 and found the appropriate number there. If necessary, the Schedules could be checked again for a period number for the literature in question. In practice, steps one and three were not difficult, but the second step was. The classifier had to choose from a variety of citation orders, depending, of course, upon the work being classified.... Directions were correspondingly complex, and all of the above considerations had to be kept in mind as one solved the puzzle (Comaromi 1976, 587–88).

Still, the Comaromi survey showed that 89 percent of the classifiers claimed to handle literature according to the prescribed method (Michael 1976, 54). *DDC 19* polished up its instructions. As one reviewer says:

> *Table 3* has comprehensible instructions at last, and has sprouted a sub-table which appears to provide even more scope for synthesis than in ·DDC 18. It is intriguing to reflect that DDC still goes overboard for far more synthesis in the horribly named "belle-lettristic arts" than in any other area: is it really logical to be able to say "criticism of the treatment of gardens in 19th century French drama written in Belgium" but to be unable to say "employment services for the mentally ill"? (Butcher 1979, 7).

By "logical" we take the critic to mean reasonable. And, of course, it is not reasonable that intense analysis of works of the imagination—works that reveal an unreal world, do not forget—is done when intense analysis of the real world is not.

It is important that the classifiers using DDC remember the application of the Tables: 3-A is for individual authors, 3-B for more than one author, and 3-C for a topic in literature or literature focused on specific persons. The Manual provides guidance to novices still learning how to handle literature.

Outline and Details of Class 800

800	Literature (Belles-lettres) and rhetoric
810	American literature in English
820	English and Old English (Anglo-Saxon) literatures
830	Literatures of Germanic (Teutonic) languages German literature
840	Literatures of Romance languages French literature

850	Literatures of Italian, Sardinian, Dalmatian, Romanian, Rhaeto-Romanic languages Italian literature
860	Literatures of Spanish and Portuguese languages Spanish literature
870	Literatures of Italic languages Latin literature
880	Literatures of Hellenic languages Classical Greek literature
890	Literatures of other specific languages and language families

Division 800: The first section is used for the standard subdivisions of literature (801–807), of literary texts from more than two literatures (808), and the history, description, and critical appraisal of more than two literatures (809).

Divisions
810–890: The remaining sections are for literature in the various languages, with American literature in English first (810). Various European languages are next with English and Old English (820) followed German literature in its specific forms (831–838) and other Germanic/Teutonic literatures (839). Then specific forms of French literature (841–848) and Provençal (Langue d'oc), Franco-Provençal, and Catalan literatures (849); specific forms of Italian literature (851–858) and Romanian and Rhaeto-Romanic literatures (859); specific forms of Spanish literature (861–868) and Portuguese literature (869). The ancient languages are next, which are specific forms of Latin literature (871–878); literatures of other Italic languages (879); specific forms of classical Greek literature (881–888); and then modern Greek literature concludes the division (889).

Division 890: The last division covers literatures of other specific languages and language families. These are East Indo-European and Celtic literatures (891); Afro-Asiatic and Semitic literatures (892); Non-Semitic Afro-Asiatic literatures (893); Altaic, Uralic, Hyperborean, Dravidian literatures (894); East and Southeast Asia and Sino-Tibetan literatures (895); African literatures (896); literature in the North American native languages (897) and South American native languages (898); concluding with non-Austronesian languages of Oceania, Austronesian, and miscellaneous literatures (899).

The Number Building Process

Example 1. A work on contemporary American writing.

The Relative Index shows American literature in English at 810, which will be our base number.

810

When we look in the Schedules under 810, we are told the following:

> Except for modifications shown below, add to base number 81 as instructed at beginning of Table 3 ...

When we turn to Table 3 we find the following:

> Notation from Table 3 is never used alone, but may be used as required by add notes under subdivisions of individual literature or with base numbers for individual literatures identified by * under 810–890....
>
> > Table 3-A for ... an individual author
> > Table 3-B for ... two or more authors; also for rhetoric in specific literary forms.
> > Table 3-C for additional elements used in number building within 3-B ...

In reviewing the three subtables, we see that B is the best choice because the work is not about any single American author. In Table 3-B we find the specific forms, which are poetry (—1), drama (—2), fiction (—3), essays (—4), speeches (—5), letters (—6), humor and satire (—7) and miscellaneous writings (—8). Because no specific form is indicated, we will use instruction 8 in front of Table 3-B.

> If the work is not limited to a specific literary form, consult —01–09 in Table 3-B. Follow the instructions at the number selected, making use of Table 3-C when specified....

The appropriate notation seems to be —09 History, description, critical appraisal of works in more than one form.

810.9

Now for the number for contemporary American literature, we find the following under —09:

—090 01–090 09	Literature from specific periods
	Add to —0900 notation from the period table for the specific literature ...

Looking at the period table for 810, we find contemporary literature for the United States at 54 (1945–1999). According to our instructions, we add 54 to our —0900 for the classification number.

810.90054   *The Literary Bent*

Example 2.   A collection of children's poems in English.

Using the outline, we find English literature at 820 and English poetry at 821.

821

Under 821 we find the following:

Number built according to instructions under 820.1–828 and at
beginning of Table 3

At 820.1–828 we find only period tables, so the next stop is at Table 3. The
preliminary instructions indicate that the Table is made up of three subtables: *A* for
collected works of a single author, *B* for collected works of two or more authors,
and *C* for additional elements used in number building within Table 3-B. At this
point, it is better for the classifier to read the instructions for Table 3-B before continuing with the next step.

Collections of poetry are classed in —1008. Because our class number already includes the "1" designation, we just add 008.

821.008

As indicated in the Table 3 instructions, we now turn to subtable C, where we
find the following Summary:

—01–09	**Specific periods**
—1	**Arts and literature displaying specific qualities of style, mood, viewpoint**
—2	**Literature displaying specific elements**
—3	**Arts and literature dealing with specific themes and subjects**
—4	**Literature emphasizing subjects**
—8	**Literature for and by persons of racial, ethnic, national groups**
—9	**Literature for and by other specific kinds of persons**

The obvious choice here is the last one, where we find notation —9282, for
Children.

821.00809282 *A Treasury of Playtime Poems*

DDC 21 Revisions

The Summaries of 800 show considerable revisions in Edition 21, many
times resulting in references to prominent languages, thus elevating them out of
the "group."

	Summary *(DDC20)*		Summary *(DDC 21)*
800	**Literature and rhetoric**	800	**Literature (Belles-lettres) and rhetoric**
820	**English and Old English literatures**	820	**English and Old English (Anglo-Saxon) literatures**
830	**Literatures of Germanic languages**	830	**Literatures of Germanic (Teutonic) languages German literature**

840	**Literatures of Romance languages**	**840**	**Literatures of Romance languages French literature**
850	**Italian, Romanian, Rhaeto-Romanic**	**850**	**Literatures of Italian, Sardinian, Dalmatian, Romanian, Rhaeto-Romanic languages Italian literature**
860	**Spanish and Portuguese literatures**	**860**	**Literatures of Spanish and Portuguese languages Spanish literature**
870	**Italic literatures; Latin**	**870**	**Literatures of Italic languages Latin literature**
880	**Hellenic literatures; Classical Greek**	**880**	**Literatures of Hellenic languages Classical Greek literature**
890	**Literatures of other languages**	**890**	**Literatures of other specific languages and language families**

A small number of modifications were made in the 800 Schedule; however, a few are quite substantive. There has been a major shift in literatures of specific languages and language families (810–890), which consist of texts of literatures of two languages (808.8) and History, description, critical appraisal of literatures of two languages (809) now found with the specific languages. In addition, the Period Tables have been revised.

808.1   Theory, technique, history of criticism of poetry (801.951) has been moved here.

808.2   Theory, technique, history of criticism of drama (801.952) is now found here.

808.3   Theory, technique, history of criticism of fiction (801.953) has been shifted here.

808.4   Theory, technique, history of criticism of essays (801.954) has been moved here.

808.5   Theory, technique, history of criticism of speeches (801.955) has been moved here.

808.6   Theory, technique, history of criticism of letters (801.956) has been moved here.

808.7   Theory, technique, history of criticism of humor and satire (801.957) has been moved here.

839   Comprehensive works on Old Low Germanic literatures (839.1) are now found here under Other Germanic (Teutonic) literatures.

839.1   Yiddish literature (839.09) is now located here.

839.2	Frisian literature now includes Old Frisian literature (839.1).
839.31	Dutch literature now includes Old Low Franconian literature (839.1).
839.4	Low German (Plattdeutsch) literature now includes both Old Low German and Old Saxon literature (839.1).
891.49	Nuristani (Kafiri) literature (891.499) is now found here under Other Indo-Aryan (Indic) literatures.
891.497	Romany literature (891.499) has been moved here.
891.56	Dari literature (891.55) is now found here.
891.57	Tajik literature (891.59) has been moved here.
891.59	Pamir literatures (891.593) is now found here under Other modern Iranian literatures.
891.86	Moravian dialects (891.87) is now included here under Czech literature.
895.4	Literatures in Himalayan languages, excluding Kiranti and Newari languages (895.49), is now located here under Tibeto-Burman literatures Tibetan literature.
899.993	Subdivisions of Interlingua literature (899.99301–.9938) are eliminated and those aspects are now located here under Interlingua literature.

Exercises in the Use of Class 800

Using your own skills, assign classifications to the following books; then, check your classifications against the class numbers in the "Answers to the Exercises" section in the appendix.

1. Autobiographies of homeless women.
2. A novel about an American woman finding herself in Jamaica.
3. A novel about a terrorist cult in Peru.
4. A guide to writing for attorneys.
5. A collection of translated ancient Egyptian writings.
6. Contemporary Arabic prose.
7. Stories from the Vietnam War era.
8. An attack on theological determinism in Holocaust literature.

Literature Cited

Batty, David C. 1976. Library classification one hundred years after Dewey. In *Major classification systems: The Dewey centennial.* Urbana-Champaign, IL: University of Illinois Graduate School of Library Science.

Bloomberg, Marty, and Hans Weber. 1976. *An introduction to classification and number building in Dewey*. Ed. John Phillip Immroth. Littleton, CO: Libraries Unlimited.

Butcher, Peter. 1979. Dewey? We sure do! *Catalogue & Index* 55: 7.

Chan, Lois Mai. 1971. The form distinction in the 800 class of the Dewey Decimal Scheme. *Library Resources & Technical Services* 15 (4): 458.

Comaromi, John Phillip. 1976. *The eighteen editions of the Dewey Decimal Classification*. Albany, NY: Forest Press Division, Lake Placid Education Foundation.

Michael, Mary Ellen. 1976. Summary of a survey of the use of the Dewey Decimal Classification in the United States and Canada. In *Major classification systems: The Dewey centennial*. Urbana-Champaign: University of Illinois Graduate School of Library Science.

Class 900
Geography, History,
and Auxiliary Disciplines

Introduction

One might think that because history cannot change there would not be much revision in 900, besides those updates required by the constant evolution (sometimes revolution) of governments as leaders are replaced, and wars started and halted. But history can be transformed to the extent that changing philosophies can interpret the past differently. Differences also occur because the existence of governments is at the whim of humankind's aggressions and desires. Thus, a country can emerge from another (as with the former Soviet states); others can be merged following wars. Consequently, 900 will *always* change and evolve and drive classifiers mad from their constant need to revise their collections. As this book is being completed, the new president of Zaire changed its name back to Congo, a sure change for the next edition of the DDC.

Outline and Details of Class 900

900	Geography, history, and auxiliary disciplines
910	Geography and travel
920	Biography, genealogy, insignia
930	History of ancient worlds to ca. 499
940	General history of Europe Western Europe
950	General history of Asia Orient Far East
960	General history of Africa
970	General history of North America
980	General history of South America
990	General history of other parts of world, of extraterrestrial worlds Pacific Ocean islands

Division 900:   In the mnemonic manner found in the Schedules, the last class is used for geography and history of places, and the standard subdivisions of the class are found in the first division (900.1–.9), and of history alone (901–903, 905–908). Section 904 is used for collections of accounts of events, and 909 for world history.

Division 910:   Geography and travel are in the second division, with the philosophy and theory of geography and travel (910.01), then physical geography (910.02), historical and persons treatment (910.0209), and physical geography of locations in general (910.021). Standard subdivisions are next (910.2–.9) with the special topic of accounts of various travels (910.4). The next section is used for historical geography (911) and is followed by atlases, maps, and charts of the earth and extraterrestrial areas (912). Geography and travel in specific places arranged like Table 2 concludes the division (913–919).

Division 920:   Biographies of certain types of people (920.1–928.9), and genealogies, awards, seals, and identifications (929) comprise this division.

Divisions
930–990:   The rest of the class is used for history and also follows the country numbers found in Table 2. The ancient world is found in 930, and the modern world and extraterrestrial worlds in 940–990, which are Europe (940); Asia (950); Africa (960); North America (970); South America (980); Australia (994); New Zealand (993); Pacific and Atlantic islands (995–997); polar areas (998); and extraterrestrial worlds (999).

The Number Building Process

Example 1.   A work on General Custer's battle with the Sioux Indians, his last battle.

This being a work on American history, we begin by ascertaining the notation for the United States. We find that it is 73; thus, the division for the United States is 973.

973
Looking in the Schedules under 973, we find the Summary:

.1	Early history to 1607
.2	Colonial period, 1607–1775
.3	Periods of Revolution and Confederation, 1775–1789
.4	Constitutional period, 1789–1809
.5	1809–1845
.6	1845–1861
.7	Administration of Abraham Lincoln, 1861–1865; Civil War
.8	Reconstruction period, 1865–1901
.9	1901–

We know from history that the great Western expansion and resulting wars with the Plains Indians occurred in the latter part of the nineteenth century. The work indicates Custer's death was in 1876, so we look under .8 and find that date occurs in the Administration of Ulysses S. Grant, which is .82.

973.82

For the aspect of the person Custer (persons treatment), we turn to Table 1 (Standard Subdivisions) and find the following Summary:

—01	**Philosophy and theory**
—02	**Miscellany**
—03	**Dictionaries, encyclopedias, concordances**
—04	**Special topics**
—05	**Serial publications**
—06	**Organizations and management**
—07	**Education, research, related topics**
—08	**History and description with respect to kinds of persons**
—09	**Historical, geographic, persons treatment**

The next step is to look under —09 for persons treatment.

—090 05	**Serial publications**
—090 1–090 5	**Historical periods**
—091	**Treatment by areas, regions, places in general**
—092	**Persons**
—093–099	**Treatment by specific continents, countries, localities; extraterrestrial worlds**

As indicated in the Summary above, the notation —092 is to be added to our number.

973.82092 *A Story of the Custer Massacre*

Example 2. An autobiography of a Jewish girl in World War II Berlin.

The three elements of this classification are World War II (when), Berlin, Germany (where), and a Jewish girl (who). The "who" would be part of the whole, but is that "when" or "where"? In this case, the "where" is important only in relation to "when." So we must start with the notation for World War II. The Relative Index indicates that number is 940.53.

940.53

When we look in the Schedules under 940.53, we find the following choices:

.5308	World War II with respect to kinds of persons
	Class noncombatants, pacifists, enemy, sympathizers in 940.5316; class Holocaust in 940.5318

Because the "who" is a Jewish girl, the obvious notation is 940.5318.

940.5318

Now we must add the element for "where." Our summary above from Table 1 indicates that would be —093–099.

—093–099	Treatment by specific continents, countries, localities; extraterrestrial worlds
	History and description by place, by specific instance of the subject
	Add to base number —09 notation 3–9 from Table 2 ...

On to the number for Berlin, which, according to Table 2, is —43155, which is added to —09.

940.53180943155   *Outcast: A Jewish Girl in Wartime Berlin*

DDC 21 Revisions

The Summaries are indicative of the shifts found within this class.

Summary *(DDC 20)*		Summary *(DDC 21)*	
900	**Geography and history**	**900**	**Geography, history, and auxiliary disciplines**
930	**History of ancient world**	**930**	**History of ancient worlds to ca. 499**
940	**General history of Europe**	**940**	**General history of Europe Western Europe**
950	**General history of Asia; Far East**	**950**	**General history of Asia Orient Far East**
990	**General history of other areas**	**990**	**General history of other parts of world, of extraterrestrial worlds Pacific Ocean islands**

Besides the alterations also found in Table 2, 940–990 has a new Add Table for wars. Also, Collected treatment of persons (00992) is now found under 0099. References to Personal narratives of wars have shifted to 092. Finally, standard subdivisions for 949.3 Southern Low Countries and Belgium, 951 China and adjacent areas, and 964 northwest African coast and offshore islands have moved from three zeros (.0001) to two zeros (.001). Standard subdivisions of 968 Southern African/Republic of South Africa have been shifted to .0001–.0009 for southern Africa and .001–.009 for the Republic of South Africa. Historical periods of the Republic of South Africa are found in .02–.06.

The changes in Eastern Europe and the former Soviet Union have resulted in a total revision of 47 in Table 2 as well as the 974 class. Changes are so extensive that Comparative and Equivalence Tables lead the weary user.

919.904   Projected accounts of manned space flight (629.4501) are now found here under Travel on extraterrestrial worlds.

919.9204   Projected accounts of planetary flights (629.455) have been moved under Travel in planets of the solar system and their satellites.

929.1028   Auxiliary techniques and procedures of Genealogy, names, insignia (929.1072) are now found here.

929.6   Armorial bearings and comprehensive works on coats of arms (929.82) are now consolidated here under Heraldry.

929.9   Seals (929.82) are now found here under Forms of insignia and identification.

940.308   World War I with respect to kinds of persons (940.315) has been moved here.

940.5308   World War II with respect to kinds of persons (940.5315) has been moved here.

940.5475   World War II Medical services of specific countries (940.5475094–.5475099) are now 940.54754–.54759.

949.3   The Standard subdivisions of the Southern Low Countries and Belgium (.30001–.30009) have been moved to .3001–.3009.

949.502   Middle Byzantine period of Greece now includes the years 1057–1081, which was 949.503.

949.507   Greece during 1830 forward now includes 1830–1833, which was moved from 949.506.

949.5072   Greece's period of monarchy, 1833–1924 (949.506), has been moved here.

949.58   Comprehensive works on the Aegean Islands (949.9) are now found here.

949.59   The Crete region (949.98) is now found here.

949.9   Bulgaria (949.77) has been moved here.

951   The Standard subdivisions of China and adjacent areas have been moved from .0001–.0009 to .001–.009.

951.035   The Sino-Japanese War, 1894–1895 (952.031), is now found here.

956.93   Cyprus (956.45) is now located here.

959.5504   Brunei periods, 1888–1946 (959.5503) and 1946–1983 (959.5505), have been consolidated here.

959.7043   Under the Vietnamese War, 1961–1975, the war with respect to kinds of persons (959.70431) has been moved to 959.704308 and Personal narratives (959.70438) to 959.7043092.

964	Standard subdivisions of Northwest African coast and offshore islands (.0001–.0009) are now .001–.009
968	Standard subdivisions of Southern Africa (.001–.008) have been moved to .0001–.0008, and Areas, regions, places, and persons of southern Africa (.009) are now found at .0009. The Standard subdivisions and Areas, regions, places, persons of the Republic of South Africa are 968.001–.009.
968.048	South African War with respect to kinds of persons (968.0481) is now found in 968.04808, and Personal narratives (968.0488) are found in 968.048092 under Persons.
973.3	The American Revolution and Confederation, 1775–1789, in relation to kinds of persons (973.315) has been moved to 973.308 and Personal narratives (973.38) to 973.3092.
973.52092	Personal narratives of the War of 1812–1815 (973.528) have been moved here under Persons.
973.62092	Personal narratives of the Mexican War, 1845–1848 (973.628), are now found here.
973.708	Civil War with respect to kinds of persons (973.715) has been shifted here.
973.89092	Personal narratives of the Spanish-American War, 1898 (973.898), are now found here.
981.01	Prehispanic period to 1500 (981.012) is now located here under Early history to 1500.
981.031	Brazilian period of European explorations, 1500–1533 (981.013), has been moved here.
981.032	Brazil, 1533–1549, which was 981.02, is now included here.
981.063	The period of 1964–1967 (981.062) has been moved here under military presidents.
981.064	The Administration of José Sarney, 1985–1990 (981.063), has been moved here under 1985 to present.

Exercises in the Use of Class 900

Now try your own skills at classifying in the 900 class by developing classification numbers for the following books; then, review your choices against the class numbers in the "Answers to the Exercises" section in the appendix.

1. A work on traveling the Colorado River from its beginning to its end in the early nineteenth century.
2. A work on discovering what is good and what is bad in Savannah, Georgia.
3. An autobiography of a Panamanian dictator in the late twentieth century.
4. A history of the Russian Revolution.

5. A work on military intelligence in the Civil War.
6. A work on the Mississippi flood of 1927.
7. A work on the Lewis and Clark expedition.
8. An African American's life with a white mother in New York City.
9. A work on the relationship of Palestinian Arabs and Israeli Jews.
10. A work on Native American tribal life and law.

15

Book Numbers

Introduction

Now that the DDC classification number is assigned, the next step is to establish a book, or author, number. In this chapter two different book number schemes are described, with examples illustrating them. The two types are Cutter-Sanborn numbers and Library of Congress author numbers. Besides these two approaches, many local or homemade systems of book number codification are often used. It should be remembered that any system of book numbers will have to be adjusted to *fit* into an individual library's shelf list to maintain the desired shelf order. A more extensive discussion of this problem can be found in Bohdan S. Wynar's *Introduction to Cataloging and Classification* (1992, 373–81).

The Functions of Book Numbers

The DDC number by itself is not sufficient to identify a work from others in the same class. The book number is a notation used to create a shelf location for each work in a library. This number is composed of a *call number,* which is composed of a *classification number* (if classified) and an *author notation,* which also may be called a book number or cutter number. It is possible, or even very likely, that several books in a library will be classified in the same DDC number. So it is necessary to use the author number to create this call number. The initial letter in the book number is usually the first letter of the author's surname or the first letter of the main entry.

The most obvious function of a book number is to create a unique call number for each work in a library; however, other purposes have been pointed out by Bertha R. Barden in her manual *Book Numbers* (1937, 9):

1. To arrange books in order on the shelves
2. To provide a brief and accurate call number for each book
3. To locate a particular book on the shelves
4. To provide a symbol for charging books to borrowers
5. To facilitate the return of books to the shelves
6. To assist in quick identification of a book when inventories are taken

Book Number Schemes

Cutter Tables

The most popular book number scheme used with the DDC was devised by Charles Ammi Cutter. The notations are called cutter numbers, and assigning them is referred to as "cuttering" or "to cutter." The most commonly used version of the Cutter scheme is the *Cutter-Sanborn Three-Figure Author Table,* altered and fitted with three figures by Kate E. Sanborn. The original Cutter table had only two figures.

The Cutter table consists of two or more initial letters from a surname or a surname and a three-digit number. Letters *E, I, J, K, O, U, Y,* and *Z* are followed by two-digit numbers. The table is arranged as follows:

Bem	455
Ben	456
Benc	457
Bend	458
Bendo	459
Chandl	455
Chandler, M.	456
Chanl	457
Chann	458
Chant	459

The numbers on the right apply to the letters in each adjoining column. The cutter number includes the initial letter of the author's name and then the number. Find the letter group nearest the author's surname and combine the initial letter with the numbers. If the author's name "fits" between two cutter numbers, use the first listed in the Schedule: Bendix is B458, *not* B459. Because it falls between Bend and Bendo, the *first* of these is used. Thus:

Bemis	B455
Benat	B456
Bendix	B458
Chandler, L.	C455
Chandler, M.	C456
Channing	C458

Work marks, or work letters, are commonly used with cutter numbers to help maintain alphabetical order on the shelves and to create a unique call number for each work. The work mark is usually the first letter of the title of the work, including articles. The work mark comes *after* the book or cutter number. Thus, the call number for James Michener's *Hawaii* would be as follows:

813.5
M623h

To maintain alphabetical order, it is sometimes necessary to use two letters from the title. Thus, Michener's *Caravans* and his *Centennial* would have these work marks:

813.5   813.5
M623c   M623ce
or
M623ca

In many libraries it is a policy to classify the literary works of authors with books *about* the author and his or her works. The books *by* an author are generally placed before the works *about* the author and his or her works. Usually a letter from the end of the alphabet is placed after the cutter or book number, followed by the initial of the author of the biography or criticism. Thus, Arthur Day's *James A. Michener*, which is a critical study of Michener's work, could be classified as follows:

813.5
M623zD

Using the *z* ensures that the criticism will stand after all other works by Michener.

Another commonly used work mark identifies different editions of a work. For this purpose, either the date can be placed in the call number or a number can be placed after the work mark. Thus, if a library happened to have three different editions of Michener's *Hawaii,* the editions would be distinguished as follows:

813.5   813.5   813.5
M623h   M623h2   M623h3
                         or
813.5   813.5   813.5
M623h   M6233h   M623h
                         1970   1972

The use of work marks is a matter of cataloging policy in each library. Their use and application vary from library to library depending on the size of the collection and the patrons. In all cases, work marks should be kept simple and should not be confusing.

Library of Congress Author Numbers

The author notations used with the Library of Congress classification can also be used with the DDC. The author number consists of the initial letter of the author's name or main entry followed by a number derived according to the directions given in the tables that follow. The numbers are used decimally.

1. After the initial letter **S**,

for the second letter:	a	ch	e	h,i	mop	t	u
use number:	2	3	4	5	6	7-8	9

2. After the initial letters **Qu**,

for the third letter:	a	e	i	o	r	y
use number:	3	4	5	6	7	9

>   for names beginning **Qa–Qt**
>   use numbers: 2–29

3. After other initial consonants,

for the second letter:	a	e	i	o	r	u	y
use number:	3	4	5	6	7	8	9

4. After initial vowels,

for the second letter:	b	d	l,m	n	p	r	s,t	u-y
use number:	2	3	4	5	6	7	8	9

If the letters in a name do not appear in the tables, use the letter closest to it. Using this system, which is only a general outline, an author could have different author numbers for works classified in different DDC numbers. The following examples illustrate the application of these rules:

1. Names beginning with the letter *S:*

Sabine	.S2	Seaton	.S4	Steel	.S7
Saint	.S2	Shank	.S5	Storch	.S7
Schaefer	.S3	Shipley	.S5	Sturges	.S8
Schwedel	.S3	Smith	.S6	Sullivan	.S9

2. Names beginning with the letters *Qu:*

Quabbe	.Q3	Quick	.Q5	Qureshi	.Q7
Queener	.Q4	Quoist	.Q6	Quynn	.Q9

3. Names beginning with other consonants:

Carter	.C3	Cinelli	.C5	Crocket	.C7
Cecil	.C4	Corbett	.C6	Croft	.C7
Childs	.C5	Cox	.C6	Cullen	.C8
				Cyprus	.C9

4. Names beginning with vowels:

Abernathy	.A2	Ames	.A4	Arundel	.A7
Adams	.A3	Appleby	.A6	Atwater	.A8
Aldrich	.A4	Archer	.A7	Austin	.A9

Conclusion

Each library will decide which book number system is the most appropriate for their collection and their users. Whether it is LC's, the Cutter tables, or another established or homegrown system, the method chosen must be carefully followed for each call number assigned so that a logical arrangement of call numbers is achieved.

It should be noted that, as in other things, "rules are made to be broken." Many libraries must sacrifice "unique" call numbers for various reasons and, because of a lack of staff or to expedite the process, decide to simplify the assignment of book numbers despite the fact that all copies of a work, and even works by different authors, will have the same shelf location. In a recent tour of libraries the author found that a public school library added just the first three letters of the main entry, which is the author's surname or the title of there is no author.

For example, for a series "Power of Algebra," the following call number was used:

512
POW

Two libraries that were part of two different large public library systems with centralized cataloging and processing use similar methods. One library used:

364.106
FR

for authors' names starting with Fre, Fra, and Fri.

The other library used:

690	690
C	C
1989	1993

for title Complete ... and author Case.

What is appropriate for one library may not be for another, so the cataloger or classifier should use the method of creating call numbers that is most suitable for the library's collection, patrons, or even the staff.

Literature Cited

Barden, Bertha R. 1937. *Book numbers: A manual for students with a basic code of rules.* Chicago: American Library Association.

Cutter-Sanborn Three-Figure Author Table. Swanson-Swift Revision, 1969. Dist. by Libraries Unlimited, Inc.

Wynar, Bohdan S. 1992. *Introduction to cataloging and classification.* 8th ed. by Arlene G. Taylor. Englewood, CO: Libraries Unlimited.

Select Bibliography

Bequet, B. and C. Hadjo Poulou. 1996. Les collections en libre acces de la Bibliothèques Nationale de France: Organisation par de partement et usage de la Dewey. *Bulletin de Bibliothèques de France* 41 (4): 40–46.

Berman, Sanford. 1980. DDC 19: An indictment. *Library Journal* 105 (5): 585–89.

———. 1989. DDC 20: The scam continues. *Library Journal* 114 (15): 45–48.

Campbell, Nancy. 1994. Dewey 101: Melvil Dewey, the Dewey Decimal Classification, and Forest Press. *OCLC Newsletter* 207: 12–20.

Caraco, A. 1997. Respect des traditions ou analyse des besoins? *Bulletin des Bibliothèques de France* 42 (5): 56–59.

Chan, Lois M. 1972. Dewey 18: Another step in the evolutionary process. *Library Resources & Technical Services* 16 (3): 383–99.

Chan, Lois M., John P. Comaromi, and M. P. Satija. 1971. The form distinction in the 800 class of the Dewey Decimal Scheme. *Library Resources & Technical Services* 15 (4): 458–71.

———. 1994. *Dewey Decimal Classification: A practical guide.* Dublin, OH: Forest Press.

Coates, E. J. 1995. BC2 and BSO: Presentation at the Thirty-Sixth Allerton Institute, 1994 session on preparing traditional classifications for the future. *Cataloging & Classification Quarterly* 21 (2): 59–67.

Cochrane, Pauline A., and Karen Markey. 1985. Preparing for the use of classification in online cataloging systems and in online catalogs. *Information Technology and Libraries* 4: 91–111.

Collins, W. P. 1993. Classification for materials on the Baha'i religion: A "B200" schedule based on the Dewey Decimal Classification. *Cataloging & Classification Quarterly* 16 (4): 103–21; 18 (2): 71–86.

Comaromi, John P. 1976. *The eighteen editions of the Dewey Decimal Classification.* Albany, NY: Forest Press.

———. 1981. *Book numbers: A historical study and practical guide to their use.* Littleton, CO: Libraries Unlimited.

Comaromi, John P., and Mohinder Satija. 1983. *Brevity of notation in Dewey Decimal Classification.* New Delhi, India: Metropolitan.

Couture-Lafleur, R. 1995. Monsieur Dewey parle maintenant français. *Documentation et Bibliothèques* 41 (1): 53–54.

Davis, S. W. 1994. Classification workbook for small libraries: Using the abridged Dewey Decimal Classification (Ed. 12). *Library Journal* 119 (4): 126.

DeHart, Florence E., and Marylouise D. Meder. 1987. Structure in computer science: DDC reflections. *Technical Services Quarterly* 4 (3): 41–54.

Dewey, Melvil. 1985. *Dewey Decimal Classification: 004–006 data processing and computer sciences and changes in related disciplines, revision of edition 19*. Prepared by Julianne Beal. Albany, NY: Forest Press.

Dodd, D. G. 1996. Grass-roots cataloging and classification: Food for thought from World Wide Web subject-oriented hierarchical lists. *Library Resources & Technical Services* 40 (3): 275–86.

Donovan, Peter W. 1975. Mathematics in a major library using the Dewey Decimal Classification. *Australian Academic and Research Libraries* 6 (2): 87–91.

Duncan, E. E. 1990. Using the DDC in online catalogs. In *Annual review of OCLC research, July 1989–June 1990*. Dublin, OH: OCLC.

Finni, John J., and Peter J. Paulson. 1987. The Dewey Decimal Classification enters the computer age: Developing the DDC Database and Editorial Support System. *International Cataloguing* 16 (4): 46–48.

Gray, R. 1982. Disasters: Natural, nuclear, and classificatory. *RQ* 44: 42–47.

———. 1986. Are there serendipitous rewards in browsing in Dewey-classified libraries? *Journal of Educational Media and Library Science* 24 (1): 22–37.

Humphry, John A., and J. Kramer-Greene. 1984. The DDC and its users: Current policies. *Reference services and technical services: Interactions in library practice*. New York: Haworth Press.

Jelinek, Marjorie. 1980. Twentieth Dewey: An exercise in prophecy. *Catalogue & Index* 58: 1–2.

Lessard, S. 1993. Pour la documentation en entomologie: LCC ou DDC? *Documentation et Bibliothèques* 39 (1): 7–10.

Liu, Songqiao, and Elaine Svenonius. 1991. DORS: DDC Online Retrieval System. *Library Resources & Technical Services* 35 (4): 359–75.

Markey, Karen. 1985. Subject-searching experiences and needs of online catalog users: Implications for library classification. *Library Resources & Technical Services* 29: 34–51.

Markey Drabenstott, Karen, and Anh N. Demeyer. 1986. *Dewey Decimal Classification online project. Evaluation of a library schedule and index integrated into the subject searching capabilities of an online catalog*. Dublin, OH: OCLC.

———. 1987. Searching and browsing the Dewey Decimal Classification in an online catalog. *Cataloging & Classification Quarterly* 7 (3): 37–68.

Markey Drabenstott, Karen, Anh N. Demeyer, Jeffrey Gerckens, and Daryl T. Poe. 1990. Analysis of a bibliographic database enhanced with a library classification. *Library Resources & Technical Services* 34 (2): 179–98.

McKinlay, John. 1973. Dewey and mathematics. *Australian Academic and Research Libraries* 4 (3): 105–11.

Micco, M., and Xiangyu Ju. 1993. Improving intellectual access to material: An online browser for the Dewey Decimal Classification System. In *Proceedings of 3rd ASIS SIG/CR Classification Research.* Medford, NJ: Learned Information.

Mitchell, J. S. 1995. DDC 21 and beyond: The Dewey Decimal Classification prepares for the future. *Cataloging & Classification Quarterly Conference* 21 (2): 37–47.

———. 1995. Options in the Dewey Decimal Classification system: The current perspective. *Cataloging & Classification Quarterly* 19 (3/4): 89–103.

———. 1996. Dewey Decimal Classification: Knowledge organization tool for the 21st century. *OCLC Newsletter* 222: 32–36.

New, G., and R. Trotter. 1996. Revising the life sciences for Dewey 21. *Catalogue & Index* 121: 1–6.

O'Neill, E. T., M. Dillon, and D. Vizine-Goetz. 1987. Class dispersion between the Library of Congress Classification and the Dewey Decimal Classification. *Journal of the American Society for Information Science* 38 (3): 197–205.

Paulson, Peter J. 1994. Dewey Decimal Classification past, present and future: An interview with Peter J. Paulson. *Library Times International* 10 (4): 49–50.

Podell, D. 1994. A date with progress. *School Library Journal* 40 (4): 52.

Rollett, K. 1996. The development of —93, the Dewey number for New Zealand. *New Zealand Libraries* 48 (5): 89–93.

Rooke, Su. 1987. From 001–006: Implementing the new Dewey schedules. *Catalogue & Index* 86: 6–8.

Schultz, Lois. 1989. Designing an expert system to assign Dewey Classification numbers to scores. In *National Online Meeting. Proceedings 1989, New York, 9–11 May 1989.* Medford, NJ: Learned Information.

Soltani, P. 1996. Translation and expansion of classification systems in the Arab countries and Iran. *International Cataloguing and Bibliographic Control* 25 (1): 13–15.

Soudek, Miluse. 1980. On the classification of psychology in general library classification schemes. *Library Resources & Technical Services* 24 (2): 114–28.

Svenonius, Elaine. 1983. Use of classification in online retrieval. *Library Resources & Technical Services* 27: 76–80.

Tait, James A. 1972. Dewey Decimal Classification: A vigorous nonagenarian. *Library Review* 23 (6): 227–29.

Trotter, R., and S. Woodhouse. 1993. On the road with DDC. *Cataloguing & Index* 110: 6–8.

———. 1995. Electronic Dewey: The CD-ROM version of the Dewey Decimal Classification. *Cataloging and Classification Quarterly* 19 (3/4): 213–34.

———. 1997. Dewey 21: A personal view. *Select Newsletter* 20: 4–5.

van der Merwe, M. S. 1989. Adaptation of the Dewey Decimal classification system in South African libraries. *South African Journal of Library and Information Science* 57 (1): 34–44.

———. 1990. Comments on Dewey 20. *Mousaion* 8 (1): 22–31.

Vizine-Goetz, D. 1994. Cataloguing productivity tools. *OCLC Systems and Services* 10 (4): 31–35.

Wiegand, Wayne A. 1996. Dewey declassified: A revelatory look at the "irrepressible reformer." *American Libraries* 27 (1): 54–60.

———. 1996. *Irrepressible Reformer: A biography of Melvil Dewey.* Chicago: American Library Association.

Will, L., and S. Will. 1997. Dewey for windows. *Electronic Library* 15 (3): 192–95.

Yi, H., and Z. Jin. 1996. The Dewey Decimal Classification in China. *Knowledge Organization* 23 (4): 213–15.

Appendix:
Answers to the Exercises

Chapter Five—Class 000 Generalities

1.	*Dewey Decimal Classification and Relative Index*	025.431
2.	*International Books in Print*	018.4
3.	*Using the World Wide Web and Creating Home Pages*	025.04
4.	*Costing and Pricing in the Digital Age*	025.11
5.	*Whitaker's Books in Print*	015.4
6.	*Implementing an Automated Circulation System*	025.60285
7.	*Win32 Programming*	005.268
8.	*Inner Loops*	005.265
9.	*The Dylan Reference Manual*	005.133
10.	*OpenGL Programming for Windows 95 and Windows NT*	006.6

Chapter Six—Class 100
Philosophy, Paranormal Phenomena, Psychology

1.	*How Could You Do That?!*	170.44
2.	*The Managed Heart*	152.4
3.	*Yoga: Discipline of Freedom*	181.452
4.	*Love's Body*	150.1952
5.	*A 3rd Serving of Chicken Soup for the Soul*	158.12
6.	*Castles Burning*	150.195092

Chapter Seven—Class 200 Religion

1.	*Southern Cross: The Beginnings of the Bible Belt*	277.5081
2.	*Early Daoist Scriptures*	299.51482
3.	*Marketing the Menacing Fetus in Japan*	291.380952
4.	*Tantric Visions of the Divine Feminine*	294.52114
5.	*The Creationists*	231.765
6.	*The Taoist Body*	299.514

Chapter Eight—Class 300 Social Sciences

1.	*Asphalt Nation*	303.4832
2.	*Spirits of the Passage*	326.09182
3.	*The Truth About Money*	378.198

4. *The Last Plantation: Color, Conflict, and Identity*   305.800973
5. *The Millionaire Next Door*   332.0973
6. *A Woman Scorned: Acquaintance Rape on Trial*   364.15120973
7. *Spies Without Cloaks: The KGB's Successors*   363.2830947
8. *Bound Feet and Western Dress*   305.420951
9. *Main Justice*   363.230973
10. *Journey into Darkness*   363.25923
11. *Sleepers*   364.1066097471
12. *Using the Internet, Online Services and CD-ROMs
     to Write Research and Term Papers*   371.302812

Chapter Nine—Class 400   Language

1. *Portuguese: A Complete Course for Beginners*   469.82421
2. *Russian: Mastering the Basics*   491.782421
3. *Swahili*   496.392824
4. *Pronouncing Dictionary of Proper Names*   423.1
5. *Handbook of Pronunciations*   421.54
6. *Acronyms, Initialisms, and Abbreviations
     Dictionary*   423.1
7. *The Oxford-Hachette French Dictionary*   443.21
8. *The Oxford Russian Dictionary*   491.73

Chapter Ten—Class 500
Natural Sciences and Mathematics

1. *The Geology of Earthquakes*   551.22
2. *Project 2061*   507.1273
3. *Science Fair Projects*   520.78
4. *From Print to Electronic: The Transformation
     of Scientific Communication*   501.4
5. *Fanfare for the Earth*   551.7
6. *The Forgotten Ape*   599.8844
7. *The Behavior Guide to African Mammals*   599.051096
8. *The Jepson Manual*   581.9794
9. *Microcosmos*   576.8
10. *Picturing Plants*   581.0222

Chapter Eleven—Class 600
Technology and Applied Sciences

1. *Dogbert's Top Secret Management Handbook*   658.302
2. *James Herriot's Favorite Dog Stories*   636.089092

3. *Men Are from Mars, Women Are from Venus*   646.78
4. *Sleep Thieves*   612.821
5. *Who Gave Pinta to the Santa Maria?*   616.9883
6. *Grands Vins*   641.22094471
7. *Migraine*   616.857
8. *What Machines Can't Do*   658.514

Chapter Twelve—Class 700
The Arts   Fine and Decorative Arts

1. *Bad as I Wanna Be*   796.323092
2. *American Visions*   709.73
3. *In the Country of Country*   781.6420973
4. *Kasparov Versus Deep Blue*   794.172416
5. *Toward a Simpler Way of Life*   720.97940934
6. *The Skirball Museum Collections and Inaugural Exhibition*   708.19494
7. *Richard Neutra and the Search for Modern Architecture*   720.92
8. *Bay Area Figurative Art*   709.794607473
9. *African American Art and Artists*   704.0396073
10. *Garrett Eckbo: Modern Landscape for Living*   712.092
11. *Four More Screenplays by Preston Sturges*   791.4375

Chapter Thirteen—Class 800
Literature (Belles-Lettres) and Rhetoric

1. *I Have Arrived Before My Words*   818.5080809206086942
2. *How Stella Got Her Groove Back*   813.54
3. *The Dancer Upstairs*   823.914
4. *The Lawyer's Guide to Writing Well*   808.06634
5. *Ancient Egyptian Literature*   893.1
6. *Men, Women, and God(s)*   892.736
7. *The Wars We Took to Vietnam*   810.9358
8. *Foregone Conclusions*   809.93358

Chapter Fourteen—Class 900
Geography, History, and Auxiliary Disciplines

1. *River: One Man's Journey Down the Colorado, Source to Sea*   917.9130453
2. *Midnight in the Garden of Good and Evil*   975.8724
3. *America's Prisoner*   972.87053092

4.	*A People's Tragedy*	947.083
5.	*The Secret War for the Union*	973.785
6.	*Rising Tide*	977.03
7.	*The Undaunted Courage*	917.804
8.	*The Color of Water*	974.71004960730092
9.	*Intimate Enemies*	956.94054
10.	*Braid of Feathers*	973.0497

Index